The Essex &
Suffolk Stour
A HISTORY

The Essex & Suffolk Stour

A HISTORY

SEAN O'DELL

TEMPUS

For my sister Chaeron
1951–1989
with love

First published 2006

Tempus Publishing Limited
The Mill, Brimscombe Port,
Stroud, Gloucestershire, GL5 2QG
www.tempus-publishing.com

© Sean O'Dell, 2006

British Library Cataloguing in Publication Data.
A catalogue record for this book is available from the British Library.

ISBN 0 7524 3911 1

Typesetting and origination by Tempus Publishing Limited.
Printed in Great Britain.

Contents

Acknowledgements

I am very grateful to all of those who have, in a variety of different ways, helped me with this project. In particular I should like to acknowledge the help and support of my wife Nicola and my children Patrick and Kate, who have patiently accompanied me on an inordinate number of trips to locations along the length of the River Stour Navigation. The River Stour Trust – in particular Anthony Platt, Lesley Ford-Platt, Ron Abbot, Doug Barret, John Osbourne and David Rayner – have been of great help by making available to me their archives and photographs, as well as their own considerable knowledge. Michael Hills, the Sudbury town council archivist, assisted me greatly with information regarding the River Stour Navigation Co.'s records both before and after they left Sudbury. Peter Minter, of the Bulmer Brick and Tile Co., helped with valuable information regarding the brick-making industry around Sudbury during the nineteenth century. The staff at the Essex County Record Office, the Suffolk County Record Office at Ipswich and Bury St Edmunds, and the National Archives, in Kew, were most helpful. From the University of Cambridge, Dr Evelyn Lord and Peter Bysouth also deserve special thanks for their encouragement and critical appraisal of my research work. Thanks are also due to John Simpson at Autograph Media (www.autograph.uk.com) for photography at Mistley, Manningtree, Flatford and Dedham.

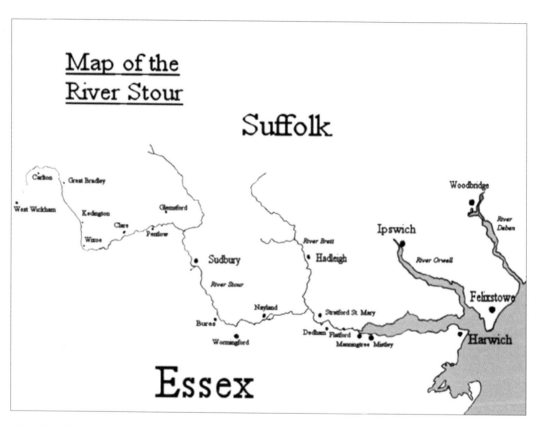

Map of the River Stour.

About the Author

Sean O'Dell has been interested in history and archaeology since childhood days. This, coupled with a passion for the sea, has lead to a good deal of research and investigation into maritime subjects generally, more recently looking at inland waterways. Sean runs a small marine business close to his home on the Essex coast, where he lives with his wife Nicola and their two children. A keen sport diver, he is also a professional scuba-diving instructor. More recently, he has been dividing his time between home, work and reading for a masters degree in local and regional history at the University of Cambridge.

Introduction

Within the scope of this book I have firstly sought to examine the circumstances surrounding the construction and general engineering works that occurred when first converting the River Stour along the Essex–Suffolk border into an inland navigation. Having come to view the navigation as somewhat unique amongst the inland waterways of England, it seemed appropriate to start by looking at the original stages of conversion of the peaceful rural river into a viable commercial trade route, and what effect this had on the people involved with the river at the time, as well as on the river itself. I have also tried to make some comparisons with other contemporary river navigation projects to see just how individual the Stour Navigation was in its earliest form, or whether in fact there were more factors in common with other rivers than had hitherto been apparent. Who first constructed the locks, and why? Were there any objections to the scheme? Did it cause social unrest to those that lived and worked along the river or were their lives improved with the coming of trade? The answers to these questions may well provide a good overview of a time of great change along the River Stour from Sudbury to Manningtree.

There is much published work generally describing the growth of the commercial inland waterways in Britain, mainly focusing on the construction and use of the canal system, and this work includes navigable rivers. There is also published material detailing the history of the River Stour in particular. It is hoped that this book will now highlight some of the factors that show the Stour Navigation to have been essentially unique from the outset, and to give an understanding as to why this was so. The purpose of the book is also to give an overview of the trading river in its heyday, and an analysis of its commercial decline and the subsequent restoration of the navigation. To have met with and discussed the subject with members of the River Stour Trust, who have themselves studied the history of the river over many years, has provided other sources of information, and has gone a long way to provide the answers I have been looking for (and raised some further questions that have had to be considered).

My involvement with the river began several years ago when I was asked by members of the River Stour Trust to carry out some work for them in my capacity as a diver. This was essentially maintenance and repair work on the restored lock gates at Dedham and Flatford, and also at the newly built locks at Great Cornard. Being greatly impressed with the restoration works that

Flatford Mill, now a field study centre.

The recently restored Cornard Lock.

Working at Cornard Lock, clearing debris from the base of the gates and inspecting the gates and lock chamber.

The gates of Cornard Lock.

The Stour close to Cornard Lock.

had been carried out on the river at that time, I became more interested in exploring the river's course, in particular the navigable section from Sudbury to the estuary at Manningtree. It became apparent that there were a number of places along the river where lock gates had once stood, mills had operated and barges had passed carrying their cargoes to and from the sea. In some places the remains of a towpath were visible; in others, side cuts and millponds could be seen. At Sudbury the old granary and warehouse still stand, now restored and in use as a visitor centre and theatre respectively, and the restored barge cuts and pools are also clearly visible. Dedham and Flatford are of particular interest, having changed little since the navigation's busiest times. The town of Manningtree still supports some maritime trade and the large malting works of the EDME Co. still stand by the river. All in all, this stretch of the river hinted towards an interesting and busy industrial past. I was, therefore, particularly interested in finding out who was responsible for these early works and the effects they had on the river physically, socially and economically. I was also keen to discover something of the nature and character of the early trading river, and whether it caused disruption to those who lived and worked in its vicinity or if it bought an increase in prosperity and trade. Having then started to view the Stour as a somewhat unique river, it seemed logical to further explore this idea by making some general comparisons with other contemporary river navigation schemes. The research for this produced some interesting results, reinforcing my view of the Stour as a highly idiosyncratic inland waterway, characterised by, for example, lighter crews ferrying tow horses across the river time after time due to the lack of provision for a proper towing path. Despite these and other rather unique problems, the navigation began successfully, and a relatively brisk trade continued well into the nineteenth century.

Right: The River Stour near Sudbury.

Below: Another view of the River Stour near Sudbury.

Any discussion about this period in the history of the River Stour Navigation would, of course, be incomplete without reference to the works of the artist John Constable R.A. Much of his work produced at this time gives us a unique pictorial record of life on the working river and I have included illustrations of this. Paintings produced by the artist, particularly of Flatford and Dedham (where his father was the miller), clearly illustrate working practices of the day, including: barge construction, gangs of lighters negotiating locks, and horses being ferried across the river, leaping fences that crossed the fragmented towing path.

Having examined the earlier beginnings of the Stour Navigation and the period of its early life as a commercial trade route, the focus then shifts to the years of decline and tries to understand how and why the trade on the river finally disappeared. Early discussions with members of the Trust, as well as reading of the published sources, gave the general historical narrative and context of the decline of the navigation, but detailed information seemed at first to be elusive. The impression was given of a terminal decline starting at around the middle of the nineteenth century, and finishing rather neatly with the outbreak of the First World War. Historically, the start of the decline was said to coincide with the coming of the railway to the region, and its effect on the transport of goods and coal prices. However, these historical landmarks are perhaps rather too convenient, and the actual causes of the navigation's decline are quite possibly far less obvious. In recent years the River Stour Trust have salvaged the remains of a steam-powered vessel, dating from 1862, sunk near Pitmire Lock. This was built, apparently, as an attempt to cut down travelling time on the river, in the face of competition from rail transport. Steam lighters had by then been working on the nearby rivers Gipping and Lark for some time[1]. This was the only example of its type. Several of the horse-drawn lighters were sunk at Ballingdon Cut near Sudbury, with their remains being visible for many years. This was said to have happened around the outbreak of the First World War, as the lighters may have been of use to the enemy in the event of an invasion, allowing them access along the river to Sudbury. This event seemed to be viewed as the symbolic, if not the historical final demise of the River Stour Navigation as a viable trade route. Although this all seemed quite reasonable, with tangible evidence in the form of the steam barge to counter competition from the railways, was it all quite that straightforward? Or were there more details to consider?

In order to test this possibility, I have addressed several questions regarding the decline of the navigation. First of all, when did the decline actually start? Was it a dramatic and sudden event which took the managers of the River Stour Navigation Co. at the time by complete surprise? Was it anticipated by observation of the industrial developments of the day? Or was it a slow dwindling of trade which happened over a far more protracted period, in an almost imperceptible way, to those involved? Did the start of the decline coincide with any particular changes or developments in the immediate locality of the navigation that may have had an effect on trade? Attempts have been made to ascertain the initial nature or symptoms of the decline in more detail. If purely financial, was this caused by a reduction in income due to the lowering of tolls or tariffs on the river, without significant loss of barge traffic, or was the actual barge traffic reducing, thus causing a reduction in income, which would have had the knock-on effect of driving down tariffs and tolls? If such measures as reductions in tolls did not attract trade back to the river, then this could have been the start of a kind of price-war-based decline similar to the one witnessed on the high street of the late twentieth century and beyond.

It has been important to look at the arrival of the railway in the locality of the Stour Navigation, and in what form it finally came. Was it simply a passenger service in the region, which would have had little effect on the carriage of bulk goods, therefore presenting little in the way of competition to the lighters on the Stour, or was the intention of the railway companies to directly challenge the navigation by instigating a goods service in the area? Was it the effect of the closest railway service that would have presented competition for the carriage of bulk goods or was it the effect of a more integrated regional network that could do the job far more cheaply and efficiently? Also, how long did any form of bulk goods transport by rail last in the region? With many of the former branch lines and depots now gone, it has also been important to try to discover how long any competition by rail in the locality of the navigation lasted, in order to quantify any long-term effect.

Research has also been carried out to discover what actions, if any, the proprietors or managers of the River Stour Navigation Co. took when faced with the onset of a period of decline, or in the face of obvious competition. We already have evidence of the construction of an experimental steam barge – how successful was it? Were opportunities to embrace and invest in new technology missed or squandered, or was a sustained decline inevitable despite their best efforts? This book also looks at the alternatives that would have been available at the time. Commercially, these might have included changes in the structure of the River Stour Navigation Co., such as alterations to the toll system and wages, or income from properties and so on. Technologically, changes might have included engineering work to make the river more efficient and easier for the lighters to negotiate. Comparisons in this respect with other inland navigations were considered, but this approach has to be viewed with some caution because, for example, local circumstances at the time in rural East Anglia would indeed have been very different from those, say, in the industrial north of England. The construction of canals in England during the boom time in the nineteenth century is a separate historical phenomenon to that of the conversion of rivers into more navigable waterways, which generally occurred much earlier. I have, therefore, simply included details of some of the Stour's neighbouring river navigations in the south-east of England for comparison.

The next area of enquiry was to examine the perceived final decline of the navigation in the early part of the twentieth century. What were the circumstances surrounding the sinking of the barges at Ballingdon? Was this really carried out in 1916 as a precaution against invading troops using them to help their advance inland or were there other reasons? What was the state of the finances and general condition of the Navigation Co. at this time and did the company go into liquidation? If so, when was it finally wound up? Did any barge traffic use the river after this period? It also seemed important to ascertain whether the navigation, although having undeniably passed through a period of serious decline to the point of abandonment, has in fact ever ceased as a viable trade route. Despite a period of uncertainty, as well as the activities (or inactivity) of large government organisations and their predecessors (including the Waterworks companies), the formation in 1968 of the River Stour Trust and their subsequent campaigning efforts have secured the future of the navigation for the time being, albeit not at present for commercial goods trade.

Finally, and before considering what conclusions may be drawn from all of this, attempts have been made to discover who the key personnel in the River Stour Navigation Co. were during this period, and what part they may have played individually or as a group in the management of the period of decline. Were any key single decisions made which had a lasting effect and, if so, by whom? Did the outside interests of these key figures have any effect on how the company was run and how they saw its future? Was the company under the influence of key individuals who were committed to its survival and growth, or did a committee whose members' main interests lay outside the fortunes of the Navigation Co., manage it? As a company can, in many respects, be seen as the sum total of the efforts and ideas of those that comprise it, then these factors must be considered in the overall discussion.

In order to answer the above questions, primary sources of information had to be identified and analysed. The archives of the River Stour Trust, including much of the correspondence of a founder member, the late John Marriage, proved to be an excellent starting point, giving a good insight into the general history, and in particular to the history of the Trust's activities since 1968. There was, however, insufficient information regarding the decline of the navigation, with the exception of details concerning the steam-powered barge project. The Suffolk County Record Office in Ipswich provided little that would help answer any of the key questions posed, either in the document archives or the recorded oral histories. However, one document of interest that did come to light here was the transcript of a talk given to members of the Stour Valley Antiquarian Society by a lady named H. Lott, a descendant of Willy Lott whose cottage was immortalised in the paintings produced at Flatford by John Constable, RA The cottage still stands at Flatford Mill. This document, whilst giving a good account of part of the history of the river, was more a set of personal recollections than a source of accurate data. Documents concerning the River Stour Navigation Co. began to surface at the National Archives in Kew, London. Here it was possible to start to find names of key personnel, and start to note dates concerning important landmarks such as the incorporation of the Navigation Co., and details of the winding up of the company. Returns to the Canals and Waterways board from 1889 to 1937 by the Navigation Co. proved very useful and revealing, as did lists held here on returns detailing the names of the directors and managers of the company. The next, and so far most productive, repository of primary sources for this project proved to be the Essex County Records Office. At one stage some time after 1937 the South Essex Waterworks Co. was involved in the affairs of the Stour Navigation, and this is probably the reason that some of the information may have found its way here. A considerable list of relevant documents concerning the river and the railway are shown in the online catalogue, and this includes some of the minute books of the Navigation Co. on microfilm for the main part of the nineteenth century. A discussion with the archivist for Sudbury town council revealed how, before the dissolution of the old Sudbury borough council, many of the documents and records of the Navigation Co. were held there, with the exception of some that were found at the old company office, which the then owner refused to part with. This would possibly explain some of the trading data that is missing from the record. From Sudbury, these documents (or at least some of them) headed for the Suffolk County Record Office branch at Bury St Edmunds, where the majority of the originals remain to this day.

The methods used to analyse the information from all of these sources have included firstly drawing up a timetable of key events during the period in question. This included events not just of relevance to the Stour Navigation, but also concerning the coming of the railway and other local and national events or developments. This was then compared with records in the minute books of the Navigation Co., to give a firm context within which to examine other information. The next stage was to collect as many statistics of receipts and details of cargoes carried on the Navigation as possible, plotting these in graphic form. This data provided comparable evidence to quantify exactly how, and possibly why, the decline in the Navigation Co.'s fortunes began, what effects any strategy detailed in the minute books had, and how this compared with the fortunes of the railway. All of these sources have also been used in an attempt to profile the motivation and direction of the key members of the Navigation Co. during its decline, to try to analyse the company's 'corporate identity', aims and aspirations. The external interests of the key members during the relevant period have also been investigated, as provides an insight into the nature of their commitment to the navigation.

There are, of course, areas where further research would be helpful. Circumstances were such at the time that the research for this book had to be completed within a reasonable timescale, and as such some of the more time consuming and illusive avenues of enquiry had to be somewhat curtailed. More detailed information on the outside interests of the key personnel involved in the River Stour Navigation Co., as well as more detailed records of goods carried by the railway companies at the time, would no doubt shed further light on the subject. As a consequence of this, it was of real concern that some of the conclusions reached in this book may perhaps have relied a little too heavily on statistical data from the Navigation Co.'s account and minute books, and that where this data was absent from the record one might be forced to speculate without hard evidence. But these concerns could be eased for two reasons: Firstly, along with statistical data, the minute books of the Navigation Co. also contain detailed records of many meetings that give a very good indication of the mood and general feeling of those present during critical times for the company. Also, where gaps in data occur, by analysing the minutes of the meetings either side of the missing information, one could reasonably be able to see more or less where the company was going. There is also additional documentation alongside the minute books (repair books, correspondence and so on) that helps to illuminate the subject. Secondly, the archives of the River Stour Trust would also prove to be useful in qualifying any speculation that may have been derived in this way. However, in considering the information yielded by these sources, it has also been important to realise that there may well be additional facts and information that they do not reveal, and each individual source is only a 'sample' of information from the period in question.

By identifying all of these factors and bringing the available data into comparison, along with an informed interpretation of the mood and feeling of the key personnel associated with the Navigation Co. during important periods in its history, it has been possible to begin to draw some interesting conclusions and observations regarding the development and subsequent commercial decline of the River Stour Navigation and how it stands today. There is clearly more work to be done, but hopefully the following chapters will at least further the debate and may even provoke further research.

one

From River to Navigation

On the Cambridgeshire/Suffolk border where the London clay to the east has given way to the chalk uplands south-east of Cambridge, the East Anglian River Stour rises at Wratting Common, north-east of the small village of West Wickham, at about 380ft above sea level. Nothing more than a ditch at first, then just a small stream, it meanders in a northerly direction passing the villages of Weston Green, Carlton and Great Bradley before working its way around to its main east-south-easterly course towards Kedington, east of Haverhill, and on towards Wixoe. The stream grows in size as it progresses around these villages, gathering drainage water from the surrounding farmland. Passing Clare, Cavendish, Pentlow and Long Melford, the Stour reaches Sudbury in Suffolk, at about 82ft above sea level.[2] The river has, by this stage, increased considerably in depth and width, and from here it follows its course to the tidal estuary at Manningtree. This stretch passing by Bures, Nayland, Dedham and Flatford, known as the Stour Valley, forms part of the Essex/Suffolk border and is surrounded by some of the most delightful and picturesque countryside in East Anglia. The tidal estuary at Manningtree becomes wider as it approaches the sea and the confluence with the River Orwell at Felixstowe on the northern shore, and Harwich to the south. At around 42 miles long, and from a stream little bigger than a ditch near its source, the Stour grows in size steadily along its length to its estuary where sea-going vessels are able to comfortably navigate into the port of Manningtree.

Archaeological evidence has clearly shown that most rivers in East Anglia were used as routes for the transport of goods and peoples as far back as pre-historic times and the Stour, or as it was sometimes known 'Stower' (meaning 'great river'), was probably no exception. During the early part of the seventeenth century we find the first evidence of proposals to make the River Stour, from Sudbury in Suffolk to the estuary at Manningtree, navigable for commercial trade. It would be reasonable to assume that during earlier times the river may well have been used informally for transportation of goods and other cargoes by small vessels, but there seems to be no documentary evidence of this. Prior to navigation works the river in its 'natural' state, whilst being fairly wide and deep in some stretches, was in fact quite narrow and shallow in others, and at certain times of the year became little more than a stream.

The Stour close to its source at Wratting
Common.

Just a ditch at first… then a stream.

Above: The first road bridge over the Stour. It is hardly noticeable, but soon the growing river will require considerably larger bridges to carry roads across.

Below: Raynors Bridge, near Great Bradley. Here the landowner informed me that during the First World War the Salvation Army would bring children down to the River Stour at Raynors Bridge to baptise them.

Towards Wixoe, growing considerably in size.

Opposite: The River Stour at Kedington Bridge.

At Kedington back towards Carlton.

The Stour at Clare Bridge.

The river at Pentlow Bridge towards Long Melford.

The Stour as it flows into Sudbury.

Opposite: A view of the Stour in the fields close to Sudbury.

Looking upstream close to Bures.

Opposite above: Looking downstream towards Wormingford.

Opposite below: Shallows midstream, looking towards Bures.

From Wormingford Bridge towards Stratford St Mary.

Dedham Lock as it stands today. Well maintained and fully operational, the lock chamber can be seen here with the tilting gate raised to control water levels upstream.

Dedham Mill and millpond. The Mill, now residential apartments, overlooks the Stour as it widens temporarily before continuing on its twisting course towards Flatford.

The Stour as it approaches Flatford. Flatford Lock and Mill are just beyond the bridge.

Flatford Mill, now a field studies centre, and the millpond from the lock.

Manningtree, at the Stour Estuary beyond Cattawade Bridge.

Mistley Quay, still operational. Beyond, in the distance, lie the ports of Harwich, Felixstowe and the sea.

At the time of the development of the Stour Navigation, the roads in Britain were not in a good state of repair. Passenger transport in coaches was uncomfortable and dangerous; bulk goods could only be transported in carts over bumpy roads in small loads. Daniel Defoe observed in 1724 that the road from London towards Ipswich was badly worn and rutted by wagons and carts.[3] He described the system of turnpikes that was gradually being introduced to raise funds to finance road repair and maintenance; however, waterways would for the time being offer a much more efficient alternative for bulk goods transport. In fact, at this stage land transport was three to four times more expensive than water on eight routes studied between 1780 and 1800.[4] A pack horse on a bridle path may carry up to two and one half 'hundredweight', a horse on a towpath could haul up to 30 tons on a river, or up to 50 tons on a canal.

On 3 January 1627, Arnold Spenser of Cople, Bedshire was granted a patent by Charles I, 'to make other rivers, streams and waters navigable and passable for boats, keeles and other vessels to pass from place to place,' and have the rights to use his own methods or 'engines on payment of £5 per annum to the exchequer and to retain the profits on rivers so improved for a term of 80 years.' This patent, which was originally granted for eleven years, was later extended to twenty-one years.[5] In 1634 Spenser met with Daniel Biatt, the mayor of Sudbury, to discuss the possibilities of work to make the River Stour navigable.[6] Professor A.W. Skempton describes Spenser as an 'Engineer–Undertaker' or simply an 'Undertaker,' who was also greatly involved in work to make the River Ouse navigable.[7] Undertakers at this time seem to have been reasonably wealthy individuals who had an interest in large civil engineering projects and probably also saw such schemes as yielding a good return financially.

Four years later Spenser obtained a Letters Patent for making the Stour navigable from Sudbury to the coastal estuary. He was never to carry out any work on the river before his death, and in 1658 the Corporation of Sudbury offered £5 towards a proposal by a Mr Maynard that similarly failed to come to fruition. Subsequently, the Letters Patent was assigned to Messers John Little and Benjamin Dodd, who claimed to have begun substantial work on the project around the turn of the century. This was a matter of some dispute, however, as in 1703 the Corporation of Sudbury were putting forward a Bill to go before Parliament to make the river navigable. The fact that John Little and Benjamin Dodd's petition against the Bill came to no avail suggests that their work on the river were minimal.[8]

On 16 February 1705 the Act of Parliament was passed, nominating the mayor and aldermen of the town of Sudbury, and Thomas Carter, Roger Scarlin, John Parish, Robert Girling, Henry Crossman, Robert Sparrow, Thomas Hall, Thomas Firmin, Daniel Hasel and Thomas Robinson, all of the town of Sudbury, as the undertakers. The Act was quite detailed in its final form and nominated an exhaustive list of arbitrators if the above named persons 'shall not agree amongst themselves' over the execution of the work on the river. Work was to commence by June 1708 and be completed by June 1713. Provision was made for the commissioners to oversee the work to the extent of being able to reappoint undertakers if work was not satisfactory or completed within the agreed deadlines and to settle any disputes with landowners. It was envisaged that the project would not only provide work for local labour in the construction of the staunches, wharves and excavations generally, but also 'will be beneficial to trade, advantageous to the poor, and convenient for the conveyance of coals, and other goods and merchandises, to and from the said towns and parts adjacent, and will very much tend to the employing and encrease of watermen and seamen.'[9]

The Act did have a number of omissions, which had a major effect on the progress of the navigation during the next few years. Firstly, there was no indication of how the work would be financed, and in order to raise the necessary capital shares were issued. The sum of £4,800 was raised, half of the shares being acquired by London merchant Mr Dean Cock along with a consortium of local Sudbury clothing merchants. Another London merchant, Mr Cornelius Denn, acquired the other half. The capital thus raised, the shareholders were authorised by the undertakers to commence work. The initial capital raised was soon deemed to be inadequate, and further calls were made on the shareholders. Eventually, £9,000 was raised, £2,500 being allocated to the provision of barges and warehouses, and £6,500 to be spent on the actual navigation itself.[10]

The other main omission from the 1705 Act was the provision for any form of continuous towpath along the river. This may well have been because it was envisaged that a number of sailing craft would use the navigation, as was the case on some of the other contemporary inland waterways (albeit somewhat sporadically), but was more probably because of objections from the riparian landowners. The lack of a continuous (i.e. continually running along one bank of the river, without fence 'jumps' or gates) towpath or 'haling path' was to contribute greatly to the unique nature of the working lives of the bargemen on the river.

The success of the navigation would also depend on goods being transported to and from the seaward end of the navigation at Manningtree. During the seventeenth century, shipping along the east coast was an extremely hazardous business. Sea charts, where they existed, were highly inaccurate, and thus navigation was difficult. The danger from the weather was ever present, as was the danger from pirates and enemy vessels.[11] It is recorded that in 1673 100 laden colliers coming into the port of Great Yarmouth were 'lamentably shattered' by the weather.[12] The situation was to gradually improve, with Trinity House providing better navigational marks, and protection being offered by the Royal Navy. By the start of the eighteenth century the port at Mistley, or 'Mistley Thorn' as it was known, was being developed with the help of a local landowning family. This was clearly of benefit to the new Stour Navigation, and follows a trend in expansion of some smaller coastal ports for the next hundred years or so. However, the coasting trade at Colchester is recorded as being in decline in the eighteenth century, with the inward trade dominated by coal, but becoming more dependent on the London market.[13]

two

The Early Navigation: Responses

The writings of the La Rochefoucauld brothers regarding their travels in England during 1784 and 1785 give us some interesting insights into the towns of Sudbury, Mistley and Harwich at this time, as well as the state of the roads. Mistley Quay is described as a busy small port with a shipyard in the process of constructing two frigates and regular imports of coal and corn, whereas Harwich is more involved with the cod-fishing industry and packet boats bound for northern ports and abroad.[14] Sudbury is described somewhat critically as a town of smugglers, bankrupts and people with no fortune, but as having a considerable trade in woollens and silks. These were bound for the London market, and work was readily available with at least 100 looms for silk and more for wool operating.[15] More generally during their travels the brothers observed large and dangerous cartloads of coal being hauled along the roads, noting in particular that when the River Soar was made navigable near Leicester, the price of coal fell sharply.[16] Where canals had been constructed or rivers made navigable, many cargoes (mainly coal) were observed on route.[17] There was a considerable expansion of trade at this time created by the mills bringing pressure to improve river navigations, and subsequently to build new canals to manage the need for moving bulk cargoes more efficiently. Despite the fact that the advantages of inland navigation were known during the Dark Ages and Saxon times, a new spirit of enquiry was emerging with regard to the improvement of rivers and development of inland waterways.[18]

Throughout history, change, or 'progress', has not always been welcomed by all of the people involved in, or affected by it – and river navigation works were obviously no exception. During the seventeenth century several navigation schemes were proposed and in most cases objections to them were raised. The vast majority of protests to such schemes came from the mill owners who depended on the flow of water along the river to operate their machinery and the riparian landowners who would object to their land being crossed along the riverbanks. Any objections from concerned local individuals were probably treated with lesser regard. In fact, as local labour was employed in the construction work on many such projects, the navigations were probably welcomed by the majority of the people living and working near them, as Sir Edward Ford (1605–1670) observed in 1641 in his 'Designe for bringing a navigable river from

Cattle at the banks of the Stour during the nineteenth century.

Bakers Mill Pond, Great Cornard.

Rickmansworth in Hertfordshire to St. Gyles in the fields: The benefits of it declared and the objections against it answered'. He notes:

> … first, a great multitude of poore labourers will have hereby good imployment, both in making and perpetuall repairing of the trench, and many of them yearly stipends and wages for daily overseeing and the severall parts of it, and the rowing and the sayling of the boats in it.

J.S. Hull notes in his paper on the Stour Navigation[19] that this concern for the social effects of the navigation is evident in the 1705 Act for the River Stour.

> [The navigation] will be very beneficial to trade, advantageous to the poor, convenient for the conveyance of coals, and other goods and merchandises, to and from the said towns and parts adjacent, and will very much tend to the employing and increase of watermen and seamen.

Clearly, at a time when help for the less advantaged was at best meagre, anything that would help create work and provide cheaper goods was considered important.

Sir Edward Ford also observed in his earlier work that objections such as the removal of water and fish, and the spoiling of mills, could be raised. The mill owners at first it would seem had little to gain and much to lose from such schemes, as staunches, flash locks and locks would interrupt the normal flow of the river and thereby either slow down or even stop the mill machinery from operating. These problems were not insurmountable, as mill ponds could be enlarged, side channels constructed, and other benefits such as mill owners controlling lock usage and having free transport of mill stones could be included in the setting up of the navigation proposals, in order to keep the mill owners on side. This was the case on the Stour Navigation, as the 1705 Act gave mill owners and/or millers between Sudbury and Manningtree the right of toll-free carriage of millstones and building materials to their mills.[20]

The riparian landowners' attitude to the Stour Navigation seems to me to have always been in some cases hostile. Even in more recent times there have been disagreements between the landowners and the River Stour Trust, the body who now maintain and promote the navigation.[21] The fact that the 1705 Act has, unlike the majority of other contemporary schemes, no provision for the establishment or upkeep of a haling (towing) path along the riverbank suggests that no agreements could be reached with them at the time. Although it has been suggested that some traffic was expected to be under sail, surely the physical nature of the river and experience on other inland waterways would have suggested even at the time that this would be very much in the minority. In fact, the 1705 Act simply stated, 'that it will be necessary in some places, to hale or tow up barges … by the strength of men horses engines or other means'.[22] This fairly vague and indeterminate wording, and the lack of any requirement for the riparian landowners to maintain a haling path and provide and maintain gates in the boundary fences that ran down to the river, suggests that the landowners had a powerful lobby at the time of the Act. There would have been several landowners involved along the river from Sudbury to Manningtree, giving them strength in numbers, and I would also suggest that one of their main concerns was livestock escaping from their land through gates left open.

three

The First Lock Constructions

Along with the construction of a basin, granary and warehouses at Sudbury, thirteen 'staunches' or 'flash-locks' and thirteen 'pound locks' were constructed after the 1705 Act along the river.[23] Hitherto weirs, constructed to aid mill owners and provide sufficient head of water to operate the mill, as well as to hold nets and baskets to trap fish, often impeded river navigations throughout the country. Boats could only pass the weirs if they were fitted with opening sections such as moveable boards or gates built into the structure. These 'navigation weirs' were the forerunners of the flash locks. These staunches and flash locks were by now favoured on East Anglian navigations, possibly because of the perceived 'less intrusive' effect on mill operation than pound locks, although this effect would vary with localised conditions such as the depth and width of the river in the vicinity of the mill. A staunch is effectively a single gate lock, constructed entirely of timber. A single beam or sill sits across the riverbed with two posts either side, one by each bank. A top swinging gate beam was mounted on one of the posts in such a way that it could be moved into position across the river and support a series of vertical planks, thus forming a dam, increasing the height of water upstream. The barges or 'lighters' would wait behind the staunch until the water had risen sufficiently. The planks were then removed, the upper beam swung open and the lighters would be carried by the rush or 'flash' of water over the shallow part of the river after the staunch. The effect of the backlog of water behind the staunch raising the level of water would make the upstream section navigable. When the gate was opened the 'flash' would not only temporarily increase the water level downstream for vessels passing to the coast, but also enable upstream bound vessels to be winched or hauled up over the previously shallow section to beyond the lock. Whilst being a useful aid to the problem of navigating larger vessels through shallow areas or shoals along the river, flash locks also caused a number of problems. The 'flash' of water that carried the vessel over the shallow sections would increase the downstream current in the river, and any vessels navigating in the opposite direction would have great difficulty in making progress upstream. The release of these quantities over water would also have the effect of eroding the riverbanks, in some cases causing deposition of sediment on the shallow areas, actually making them worse. The biggest drawback of the flash lock was the amount of water wasted each time it was used. This was to cause problems such as

Left: An original River Stour pound lock.

Below: The tow horse waits patiently while a lighter is worked through Flatford Lock.

vessels having to group together in order to use the locks, and instances of simply not enough water being available for extended periods.[24]

Fen lighters were known to be using their own portable 'staunching tackle' until well into the nineteenth century in order to safely navigate certain stretches of the River Nene in the vicinity of Peterborough and Wisbech. This system, said to have originally been developed and used by the Romans (as are many developments in civil engineering) on the River Lee and other inland waterways, consisted of a kit of posts, an empty boat and a canvas sheet. A temporary weir would be constructed to sufficiently raise water levels to aid navigation.[25]

Staunches can really be considered as slightly more sophisticated flashlocks, built in a more permanent manner, in some cases with a pair of gates as opposed to a single structure. The stretch of river between two staunches would raise when the upstream gates were open and the downstream ones closed (rather like an extended pound lock), and this considerably aided the movement of vessels along the navigation. Flash locks or staunches became common on other river navigations, generally in the south. In the West Country they were used on the rivers Tone, Parret, Wye, Lugg, Stour and Avon. In the Midlands the rivers Derwent, Soar and Nene made use of them as did the rivers Itchen, Arun, Ouse, Rother, Stour, Medway, Wey and Lee in the South East, along with the Thames itself. In East Anglia the rivers Great and Little Ouse, Ivel, Lark and, of course, Stour featured some of the earliest examples.

The first pound lock in England is said to have been constructed between 1554 and 1556 on the Exeter Canal by John Trew of Glamorgan, although as contemporary writers often confused pound locks with flash locks or even weirs, some doubt has been expressed over this.[26] The construction of the pound locks on the Stour was almost unique. Pound locks are the more conventional forms we are more familiar with on canals, consisting of two sets of gates and a central chamber or pound. Lighters would pass through the upstream open gates and stop in the pound before the downstream closed gates. The upstream gates would then be closed; the sluices in the downstream gates would be opened to allow the water level to lower sufficiently to open the downstream gates. Once the water level in the pound was the same as the level outside, the downstream gates would then be opened to allow the lighter to pass through and proceed along the river at a lower level. Pound locks required more intensive engineering work to install than the simple flash locks, as not only did the gates have to be constructed and installed, considerable excavations would be required around the lock site, as the river would now continue at a lower level. In fact, the effect of installing pound locks was to raise the level of water between each lock as a result of 'backlogging' the flow of water in the river, thus making it navigable for trade vessels. The pound lock gates themselves differed also from the simple single-gate flash locks in that there were two gates at each end of the pound, hinged from a land post on either side of the river and closing mid-stream, pointing toward the flow of water. For this reason they were often referred to as mitre gates. The feature that was very characteristic of the River Stour pound locks was the fact that a lintel or crossbeam was installed to take the strain of the weight of the lock gates on the land posts. The lintel spanned the river between the tops of the land posts at a height that allowed traffic to pass under, and thus prevented the land posts and heavy gates collapsing inwards under the strain. The sides of the pound within the locks were originally of an earth construction, although this was later rebuilt in timber in most cases.[27]

All locks on the first constructions after 1705 were built using timber, with fittings such as hinges, pintles, bracings and fixings of iron. The undertakers and their foremen oversaw their construction, and I would suggest this was actually carried out by local labourers, wheelwrights, carpenters and blacksmiths. The excavation work to dig out and prepare the sites alone would have been quite considerable, and in the absence of industrial machinery, would have been labour intensive. The fabrication of the gates and beams also was a considerable task, as was the

An early view of Nayland Lock.

An early view of Pitmire, or as it was sometimes known, Pitmore Lock.

job of installing them. Therefore, the local community of labourers and artisans would surely have welcomed such a considerable amount of paid work.

The original staunches on the River Stour are now almost completely gone, except for a few rotting timber remains here and there. A fairly complete example of an East Anglian staunch can be found on the Great Ouse at Castle Mills, its later brickwork intact and gates remaining.[28]

four

The Effects on the River: Physically and Socially

The 23½-mile stretch of river between Sudbury and Manningtree was, in many respects, never to be the same after the first navigation works were completed and the first lighters started to make the journey. The lighters, which would be registered with the Sudbury corporation, were built mainly in a dry dock at Flatford (still visible today), would take about two days to make the journey and would have a crew consisting of a captain (or lighterman) and his horseman. The crew was responsible for two lighters which, when chained closely together stem to stern, would be pulled the majority of the way by the horse. The lighterman would 'pole' the pair of lighters manually through areas where the horse could not access easily. There is some disagreement as to their dimensions and cargo capacity, but it is generally thought that each lighter was up to 47ft long and 10ft 9in at the beam; capable of carrying 13 tons of cargo – this was a considerable task for the horse and lighterman. The horse had to be strong, and the horseman was, in fact, most of the time a boy.[29] The problems for the horse did not end there, however, as the lack of a consistent haling path alongside the river meant that the horse would have to cross the river in total thirty-three times. With only sixteen bridges along the navigation, the problem of horses crossing the river where there was no bridge was solved in a typically unique 'River Stour' way. Horses were trained to step aboard a lighter, where they would be ferried across the river to the opposite bank, at which point they would step ashore again. This was a particularly hazardous exercise, as the slippery decks on the lighter meant that despite the lighterman placing straw down to help the horse grip on deck, the animal could easily slip and fall. Several horses are said to have fallen and drowned in the river in this way. As if this was not enough for the pitiable horses to cope with, as the riparian landowners' fences generally came all the way down to the riverbanks, they also had to jump fences at regular intervals. A large, muscular horse used for towing lighters is not best suited to leaping fences and this put even more strain on the animals concerned. Landowners were intent on keeping the 'jumps' to a height of at least 3ft, in order to keep livestock from straying into adjacent fields at first, although this height was to be lowered in due course.[30] I would suggest that the use of boys as horsemen was quite deliberate as in addition to taking a lesser wage, he would prove less of a burden as he rode the horse over fences and stiles along the way. Thus, Stour Navigation barge horses must have been the

The dry dock at Flatford, restored and maintained, this being where Stour lighters were constructed in earlier times.

A family relax aboard a River Stour lighter.

An early view of a Stour lighter 'beam-on' gives an impression of the size of these vessels.

Stour lighters in Wormingford Cut. This wonderful image shows a gang of lighters, chained stem to stern, with the lighterman in the barge furthest forward and his mate leading the tow horse.

An early view of the bridge over the River Stour at Dedham.

River Stour Lighters tied up at The Anchor Pub, Nayland.

Snowy at work towing the recently restored River Stour Trust's lighter. Stour tow horses had to be strong but agile to cope with the rigours of their journey.

fittest and strongest (capable of leaping fences and pulling two barges at a time) of any on the canals of England. Surveys made much later, in 1850, detail some 123 jumps along the navigation and twenty places where horses would have to be ferried across from bank to bank (known as 'boating places'). Even at this time – later in the development of the navigation – jumps were seen as difficult and problematical by the surveyor, citing places where trees and other obstructions were causing hazards, jumps were still too high, and even a place where horses had to swim across the river.[31]

During the period of interest, at the beginning of the working navigation, life along the river soon must have settled into a routine that was quite unique along the waterways of East Anglia, with leaping barge horses towing huge pairs of lighters, being carried across the river when there was no bridge to allow them to walk across. The meandering 'natural' river was transformed by the initial lock-building programme into a busy navigation with the lightermen and horse boys making the two-day journey, negotiating the not inconsiderable hazards along the way. The lighters would usually reach the halfway point at Horkesley by the end of the first day and a bunkhouse or 'bothy' was built there for the crew's overnight stop. The increase in the use of the river consequently bought with it an increase in trade for innkeepers as well as suppliers of feed and straw for horses, running repairs on lighters and chandlery supplies, not to mention the barge building in the dry docks at Flatford. In the places where handling the lighters was awkward, local lads would come out to help the barge crews, either leading horses, pulling on ropes or helping with lock gates.

The mill owners were probably far less happy with the state of affairs initially, and this situation would not have helped any negotiations to establish a more consistent haling path. The use of the pound locks and staunches would have disrupted the constant water supply crucial to the millers for the operation of the mill machinery, and despite appeasements such as free transport for millstones and so on, more help would be needed. Millponds were dug or extended, and side channels or weirs were constructed and the river's natural course and banks were altered further. The sites of the mills at Cornard, Bures, Wormingford, Wissington, Dedham and Flatford would have thus undergone further change and physical alteration.

Apart from early teething troubles, and despite the physical hardships associated with the work of the lightermen with their crews and horses, the navigation in its early years up to its heyday, was a commercial success. Trade became brisk and included cargoes such as oil, pitch, soap, vinegar, paper, tallow, iron, lead, sugar, butter and bricks. Wheat and other agricultural products such as flour, peas, beans, barley, oats, malt, bran and cloverseed were carried, but the first main cargo to be carried on the Stour was coal, upstream from Manningtree.[32] The demand for coal was growing generally at this time, and as trade grew for the Stour Navigation, annual cargoes of 100,000 tons were recorded.[33]

In 1781 it was necessary to pass another Act, partly to appoint new commissioners as they had hitherto not been properly elected as vacancies occurred, and partly to address some of the practical problems that had arisen along the navigation during the previous years. Among the new appointees were Golding Constable, father of the artist John, and the brothers of the artist Thomas Gainsborough, Samuel and John. Surveys were carried out and improvements made, but the essential 'fatal flaw' of no provision for a single continuous unimpeded path was never resolved.

As has already been suggested, the attitude of the riparian landowners to the new navigation was, at the very least, unhelpful, and must also be considered to be one of the factors that impeded its development and ultimately threatened its survival. It is entirely understandable that farmers and landowners would want to keep their boundaries fenced in to prevent livestock straying and keep trespassers away, but the significant problems and delays that this caused to the crews of the lighters and their tow horses was clearly not being addressed at this stage. With examples of other river navigations working around the country without these hindrances, it seems odd now (with the benefit of hindsight, of course) that some more strident efforts were not made to negotiate a more favourable haling-path system with those whose land ran down to the riverbank. The main objection to commercial traffic on the river raised in more recent times is that its presence would significantly disturb the peaceful rural nature of the river. Indeed, the Stour Valley between Sudbury and Manningtree is arguably one of the most beautiful areas of countryside in East Anglia, even to this day. It is uncertain, however, whether this argument would have held much weight during the mid-eighteenth century.

The arrival of the railways was seen in the region with the opening of the Eastern Counties Railway terminal in Colchester in 1843, heralding the start of forty years of network development.[34] These developments included the incorporation of the Colchester, Stour Valley, Sudbury and Halstead line in 1846 as being a direct challenge to the River Stour Navigation, which reputedly offered to sell itself to the railway company for £30,000.[35] This offer was refused, as was the counter offer from the railway company (see chapter 7). Local railway historical writing gives details of the subsequent development of the Stour Valley line, from its opening in 1849, its absorption by the Great Eastern Railway in 1898 and onward.[36] Other lines to Mistley and Manningtree were developed, and contemporary population figures of these towns during the development of the railways show a marked effect. Some accounts also suggest that after its offer being refused in 1846, the River Stour Navigation Co. went on to spend large sums on reducing the number of locks on the river to fifteen, and continued precariously trading coal and timber along the river with the aid of steam barges and reduced rates until 1916.[37]

five

Evidence in Art: The Works of John Constable

John Constable, RA, was born in East Bergholt, Suffolk, in 1776, the son of Golding Constable, a local mill owner. His early love of painting whilst at Dedham Grammar School continued into his early working life in his father's mill at Flatford, until he left for London to pursue his artistic career. He later said, 'I associate my careless boyhood with all that lies on the banks of the Stour; those scenes made me a painter'.[38] It has often been said that Constable's genius lies in his attention to detail and ability to capture the reality of the scene. His beautiful and dramatic skies come from this power of observation coupled with his knowledge of the weather, learned from his time at the mill with his father. Although John Constable was painting some time after the first opening and usage of the Stour Navigation, I believe he witnessed many of the factors that had come to characterise the river after, and as a result of, the 1705 Act of Parliament. His ability to record in his work the key features and details of the everyday working life on the river at places such as Dedham and Flatford have given pictorial evidence of the unique nature of the navigation.

The detail from 'The White Horse' painting clearly shows the lighterman straining on his pole as he works the lighter across to the other bank of the river. The horse is aboard and stands patiently at the bow of the lighter, attended by a lad, waiting for the moment when they must jump ashore, and continue the task of towing the lighter on its way.

'The Leaping Horse' shows a young man astride a powerful horse leaping a fence, before preparing to tow the lighter in the background on its way as before. Constable observed this sight, peculiar to the Stour Navigation, many times in his youth, along with many other details of working life along the river. For example, 'Boat building near Flatford' gives a superb image of the Stour lighter under construction in a dry dock, excavated next to the river just as it would have been around the start of the navigation construction after 1705. The boat builder works in front of a nearly complete lighter with his tools and equipment around him. A study of the full-size image reveals a wealth of information about the work of the boat builder. The dry dock is at Flatford, and has been restored by the River Stour Trust using some of Constable's drawings. The details that the artist captured have been of enormous help, from the layout of the dock to the 'chunker' or drainage tunnel that ran from the dock below the river into a lower area on the other side.

Some of the works of John Constable, RA featuring the Stour Navigation.

Above: 'The Leaping Horse'. A horse is jumping a fence by the river. Often accompanied by a boy, some horses would leap fences un-mounted.

Left: 'Boat Passing a Lock'. A detailed view of an early lock in use.

Opposite above: 'Flatford Mill'. Everyday working life on the Stour Navigation.

Opposite below: 'The Hay Wain'. Willy Lott's cottage is featured on the left of the painting.

Other evidence of daily life on the River Stour Navigation is recorded by the artist from around this time, including some superb details of the lock gates in use. 'Boat Passing a Lock' gives a view of a pound lock of the type constructed after 1705 being negotiated by a smaller vessel under sail. The construction of the lock gates is clearly shown in this work. The lock is a smaller one not requiring the characteristic lintel above the gateposts.

'The Stour near Dedham' is another example of Constable's ability to capture the work of the lightermen on the river, again using the pole to move the lighter where the horse could not pull them along.

'Flatford Mill' is a painting full of evidence of the working practices along the navigation. A lighterman is 'poling' a pair of lighters through a section of water past the locks, while his mate is preparing to couple up the horse with its towing rope. A young lad sits barefoot astride the horse to help out. A section of towpath leads back to the pound locks with their lintels above the gateposts clearly visible in the full-size image.

John Constable's paintings have provided a legacy of superb visual information about the day-to-day life on the River Stour Navigation as well as details about the construction of the locks and lighters. Like many great artists, Constable gained limited recognition from his patrons in his lifetime, but he wrote, 'I do not enter into the notion of varying one's plans to keep the publick in a good humour'. Of his art he wrote, 'The landscape painter must walk in the fields with a humble mind. No arrogant man was ever permitted to see nature in all her beauty.'[39]

six

Neighbouring River Navigations

The Essex & Suffolk River Stour was not alone amongst the rivers of eastern England to be used for transportation from early times, and to undergo subsequent improvements and 'conversion' into formal navigations. The River Lea (or Lee) from Hertford to its junction with the River Thames in London has a long history of such use, apparently being the chosen route of Viking invaders to work their way inland, wreaking havoc as far as Hertford. Improvements to the river are recorded to have taken place as far back as the fourteenth century, and during the fifteenth century an Act of Parliament was passed to provide for further improvements. Similarities with the River Stour also seem to arise from this period, as it was at this time that a board of commissioners was established to administer the navigation and, with the construction of new locks, came discontent from mill owners who perceived a threat to their livelihood. The main cargo on the river at this time was grain to supply the bread-making and brewing industries, and any lingering disputes regarding improvements to the navigation were resolved in its favour in the high court at the end of the sixteenth century.

During the eighteenth century, like the Stour, the Lea Navigation prospered, but gradually these similarities began to fade. The River Lea Navigation was now about to enter a period of increasing use and development. The nineteenth century saw a time of growing commercial traffic along the river, and with the necessary improvements including new locks and an Act of Parliament to authorise the addition of new sections – and despite competition from the railway – the navigation continued to flourish. The geographical location of the Lea Navigation (from the county town of Hertford to the capital) and the simple process of demand and supply were obviously major factors in its continued success as an inland waterway. Other factors would arguably have been the management's continual drive to see through improvements and to maintain it in good order. The increasing income that resulted was clearly of benefit to the navigation itself as well as its shareholders. By the beginning of the twentieth century, any residual similarities with the River Stour Navigation were long gone, as the River Lea Navigation now had the characteristics of a busy industrial canal rather than a rural river navigation. After the First World War a major scheme to enlarge and improve the navigation was instigated, and continued work in the 1930s would seem to ensure its future as part of the nation's commercial inland waterway network.[40]

Despite a serious pollution problem associated with its proximity to the many manufacturing sites that it served during the late nineteenth and early twentieth century, the River Lea Navigation continued to be used commercially well into the 1960s, and latterly was to become popular with leisure boat owners. Although much of its use is now recreational, the Lea is still a busy waterway, much altered and enlarged from its original natural state.

Trade and the growing demand for goods in London was the catalyst for the development of several of the smaller tributaries of the Thames, including the Roding Navigation. The most westerly of the Essex rivers entering the Thames, the Roding, or 'Rodon' as it was formerly known, Creek was navigable throughout the seventeenth century as a tidal waterway as far as Barking, and in 1736 navigation was formally extended to Ilford Bridge.[41] Unlike the River Stour, the Roding Navigation was also commercially active well into the twentieth century.

Another Essex waterway joining the Thames is the Mardyke Canal, running from Bulphan Fen, north of Grays to Purfleet. Although used as a commercial waterway, it was never officially converted into a navigation as such.

The Chelmer & Blackwater Navigation, running from the Essex county town of Chelmsford to the Blackwater Estuary, has several factors in common with the Stour Navigation, as well as some important differences. Schemes to convert the Chelmer, a small river, into a navigable waterway as far as the Blackwater – thereby linking it to the coast – were considered during the seventeenth century. An Act of Parliament was passed, but the necessary funds could not be raised for a considerable time. Again, many objections to the proposals were raised, chiefly by mill owners who, in common with their counterparts on along the Lea & Stour, saw a threat to their livelihoods. Objections were also voiced by the townspeople of Maldon, who foresaw a loss of port dues. However, by the end of the eighteenth century another Act of Parliament heralded the commencement of construction works along the proposed navigation and the formation of the proprietors into a company. The navigation was open for trade along its entire length, around 14 miles, by 1797. The main cargo along the navigation was initially coal to Chelmsford, and soon the coal merchants at the town's wharves were joined by sawmills, stone masons, lime kilns and iron works. Thus, the early part of the eighteenth century saw a brisk trade along the navigation in a manner very similar to the Stour Navigation further to the north. A diverse range of cargoes began to be carried but a gradual decline in trade is recorded form the mid-nineteenth century, after the construction of the Eastern Counties Railway from Colchester to London. However, the establishment of the first inland gasworks in Britain near the head of the navigation shortly after its opening ensured that the carriage of coal would continue well into the twentieth century. A well-established and efficient towpath no doubt aided the movement of lighters along the waterway in the early years, until powered vessels became more common. Horse-drawn lighters were in use again during the 1950s, replacing a small fleet of motorised timber lighters! During the 1960s improvements were made to the sea-lock at Heybridge Basin, allowing the now larger coastal trading vessels to enter and discharge their cargoes more efficiently onto the navigation's lighters, which were now once again motorised. In fact, timber continued to be carried along the Chelmer and Blackwater Navigation until 1972. After the final cargo of timber was unloaded at Springfield Basin, the area at the head of the navigation fell into disuse. With the prospect of the basin and locks being dismantled or filled in, the Inland Waterways Association were at the head of a campaign to restore and preserve the navigation as a whole, and these objectives have now been largely achieved.

A few miles south of the Stour, the River Colne in its tidal reaches has been accessed by trading vessels also from early times. In 1698 the stretch from Wivenhoe into Colchester at the Hythe Quay was formally made navigable, but this was really just a short extension to the already reasonably accessible tidal zone of the lower river.

Progressing northwards, the next estuary on the east coast is that of the rivers Stour and Orwell. Dividing at Shotley Point, the River Stour's tidal estuary joins the inland navigation at Manningtree and Mistley, and the River Orwell's tidal reach branches away up to Ipswich in Suffolk. It is here that the Orwell becomes the River Gipping, and the section that runs from Stowmarket down to Ipswich was, during the eighteenth century if not earlier, seen as having potential for conversion into an inland navigation. In 1790 a Bill was put forward for the Ipswich–Stowmarket Navigation, but delays caused by legal arguments were not resolved until 1793, when a second Bill was more successful. Work commenced under the direction of John Rennie, with day-to-day control supervised by Richard Coates – the same team who, at roughly the same time, worked on the Chelmer and Blackwater Navigation.[42] Consequently, the methods and approach to the construction of the navigations was very similar, and by 1794 between two and four barges were regularly working along the river. The navigation developed in a broadly similar way to its neighbour to the south, the Stour, and the trustees seemed to be quite content until the Eastern Union Railway published plans to build a line from Ipswich to Stowmarket. In a manner similar to their counterparts at the Stour Navigation, the Ipswich–Stowmarket trustees approached the railway company, in this case offering to lease the navigation to them. This would have been fine but for a provision in the Act of Parliament prohibiting the trustees leasing the navigation. Once this issue was raised it was eventually resolved, and the Ipswich–Stowmarket Navigation was duly leased to the railway company, with the condition that they would be responsible for its maintenance and upkeep. In 1888 the navigation was re-acquired by its trustees, in a considerably run-down state. Despite this, the waterway was back in service and continued to carry commercial cargoes right through until 1917.[43] After this time the waterway had more or less fallen into disuse, and in 1922 it was proposed to close it down to commercial traffic. By 1930 the powers of the trustees were revoked and the Ministry of Agriculture & Fisheries confirmed this in 1932. The Ipswich–Stowmarket Navigation was finally wound up in 1934. There are, of course, some interesting comparisons to be made here with the River Stour Navigation. The immediate consultation with the railway company upon the announcement of plans to build a line between Stowmarket and Ipswich echoes the decision by the proprietors of the River Stour Navigation to approach the Eastern Counties Railway after the proposals to build the Stour Valley line were put forward. General comparisons can also be made with the duration of the commercial 'life' of the Ipswich–Stowmarket Navigation and the Stour, although clearly a different state of affairs existed on the former navigation during the years of its lease to the railway company. The fact that neither waterway was trading commercially beyond the early part of the twentieth century, coupled with their respective relationships with railway companies in their locality, is interesting, even though other factors clearly affected each navigation independently.

Further to the north of the county, the River Blyth, through Halesworth to the tidal estuary between Walberswick and Southwold, was deemed worthy of conversion to formal navigation. Following the construction of four locks very similar to those used on the River Stour, the river was in use for barge traffic by 1760. The Blyth or Halesworth Navigation never had to contend with competition for goods carriage from a railway line along its length. In fact, after the arrival of the railway line at Halesworth, the navigation would have provided a useful link to Southwold and the coast. The big problem for this particular waterway was the constant silting up of the river around the estuary. Trade, mainly in coal, had grown steadily along the navigation from the start, but by 1840 the Southwold end of the navigation was more or less completely blocked.[44] Despite being eventually cleared, trade on the river went into decline during the second half of the nineteenth century, and by 1884 abandonment was proposed. Shortly after the Board of Trade were informed officially of the navigation's disuse, one Wherry is said to have made use of the navigation up to 1911. The navigation came to an end finally in 1934 under the Land Drainage Act of 1930.

The examination of river navigations further north into the county of Norfolk, namely the rivers Waveny, Yare and so on, presents a more complex situation. Although in several ways there are similarities with the River Stour Navigation, the network of interconnected navigation works that have come to make up the inland waterways that we know today as the Norfolk Broads are an area probably best examined in their own right. Owing to the very individual character of the evolution and development of the Broadland Waterways, there is probably less to gain in making in-depth comparisons here, and much to confuse the issue.

The same could be said about the Fenland navigations to the west, in that the need to drain the surrounding landscape was one of the key factors that brought about the engineering works that converted many of the existing rivers to navigable waterways, and therefore the evolution and development of these navigations have an additional influence that sets them apart from their counterparts to the south and east. However, an exception should be made here with the River Great Ouse as although its development as a river navigation is inextricably linked with the needs of land drainage (along with its many adjoining waterways), it has some interesting factors for comparison with the Stour Navigation.

The Great Ouse had seen changes to its size and course long before the engineers of the seventeenth century set to work, and in common with other rivers in the Eastern Counties it was probably used for navigation since the earliest times. By the beginning of the seventeenth century it was realised that action was needed to prevent further flooding of the Fens, and an Act was duly passed to recover many lost acres of land. The Great Ouse was navigable at this time as far as Huntingdon, and was used as a route for the export of agricultural produce. It seemed logical, therefore, whilst the drainage works were underway, to extend the existing navigation as far as Bedford. Arnold Spenser, before his meeting with the mayor of Sudbury to discuss making the River Stour navigable, was already setting his sights on extending the Great Ouse Navigation as far as possible. With his partner Thomas Girton,[45] they oversaw the construction of further sluices, but over the ensuing years they did not reach the ultimate goal of Bedford. With the onset of the Civil War, the navigation works fell into decline, and it was not until 1689 that the navigation was completed as far as Bedford. It is from this time that we hear of the all too familiar reports of disputes with mill owners and landowners. This seems to have been a factor that all river navigations ultimately had to deal with, and apparently the Great Ouse was no exception. Nevertheless, further development of the navigation continued, promoted by Acts of Parliament in 1751, 1795 and 1796, 1805, 1816, 1818 and 1819, 1827 and 1830. The beginning of the nineteenth century saw a commercially successful inland navigation with a well -maintained infrastructure and busy traffic in a variety of cargoes. This success was to continue well into the nineteenth century, promoting a general feeling of confidence in the navigation as viable in the long term. This general feeling was reinforced by the fact that receipts had, for some time, shown a tendency to rise steadily. This confidence was amply demonstrated on the Cam Navigation, where a 'State Barge' was constructed, and apart from one day of the year when it was used to assist the conservators to survey the navigation, it spent the rest of its time in a specially constructed dock and boathouse where an employee kept it in good order.[46] In addition, a banqueting hall was constructed from the navigation's profits and, similarly, was used only occasionally. Although this sort of extravagance did not take place on the Great Ouse itself, or indeed on the River Stour, it clearly shows the level of confidence that the proprietors had in their waterways at this particular time.

Towards the mid-nineteenth century, the Great Ouse Navigation at last started to feel the effects of competition. But in this case it was not in the form of the new railways, as was the case with the Stour, but from another waterway! The Grand Junction Canal was fully opened by 1805, and passed close by areas that had hitherto been part of the Great Ouse Navigation's catchment. A deterioration of the relationship between the proprietors and the merchants at Bedford did nothing to help matters and a decline in trade ensued. The obvious answer seemed to be joining the Great Ouse Navigation to the Grand Junction Canal, but the scheme was estimated to be prohibitively expensive. Several other schemes were proposed, and had some of these come to fruition, it is conceivable that an 'Eastern Counties' canal network could have linked the Stour, the Great Ouse and possibly some of the other river navigations in the region together, forming a far more complex and accessible waterway network for East Anglia.

With none of these schemes to link the river navigations being completed, and already trying to compete with the Grand Junction Canal, the Great Ouse Navigation was in no condition to take on further competition for goods trade from the expanding rail network. From the mid-nineteenth century the familiar pattern of lowering tolls and declining profits set in. The navigation began to be viewed by its shareholders and the local authorities whose jurisdiction it passed through as being increasingly ineffective. The navigation's towpath, although arguably more consistent than that of the River Stour, still required tow horses to jump fences, thus making journey times slow by comparison to other newer modes of transport. With shareholdings passing to individuals as opposed to groups, the navigation continued into the twentieth century in decline as far as commercial traffic was concerned, but with growing use from pleasure craft. Today the Great Ouse is essentially a pleasure craft navigation, with restored locks and a healthy interest in its history and, as always, its part to play in drainage of its surrounding areas.

seven

The Trading Years

1780–1849

It can now reasonably be suggested that the original Act of 1705 resulting in the birth of the River Stour Navigation, whilst laying the foundation for a successful trading inland waterway, did not envisage many of the problems that would hamper its growth and development. Records from this time are scarce, with the exception of a well-preserved lease document for the 'tolls of the River Stower' to 'Jasper Cullum for eleven years from Michaelmass 1741,'[47] and the fact that some of the difficulties or 'growing pains' experienced prior to 1780 appear in documented form in the National Archives as grievances from riparian landowners and mill owners. Up to six gangs of barges, each laden with twelve chaldrons of coal, are described as regularly working in a waterway that was in a state of decline and mismanagement. Staunches are described as being fixed and misused with no staunch drawer being appointed, the river filling with shoals and gravel beds, mills being spoiled and stables for barge horses falling into disrepair.[48] Consequently, the second Act of Parliament was passed during the reign of George III on 31 October 1780, amending the original 1705 Act and primarily appointing new commissioners to the navigation, as by now only two of the original remained. Other minor modifications were made but, significantly, there was still nothing in this Act to address the issue of an in-continuous haling path.[49] Not enough trading statistics survive from this early period to chart a specific detailed growth pattern, but trade must surely have developed, despite the problems, in order to necessitate the second Act.

Given the alternatives available at the time, the Stour Navigation, although twisting and turning and without a continuous towpath, must have been seen at this point as a viable and very efficient trade route. Transport of bulk cargoes by road was highly inefficient and costly, being three to four times more expensive as water on a number of routes studied up to 1800. The barges, however, were capable of holding much larger cargoes allowing bulk carriage and delivery of goods such as coal, agricultural produce, oil, bricks and lime.[50] As the sea-going

Queen's Head, Nayland Sep. 27th 1790.

NAVIGATION

OF THE

RIVER STOUR.

WHEREAS it has been found by Experience that great Inconvenience and Mifchief have arifen to the Proprietors of the faid Navigation, as alfo to the Millers on the faid Navigation, and the Occupiers of Lands adjoining thereto, by means of Barge-men, Boatmen, and others employed in towing or haling of Boats, Barges, Keels, Lighters, or other Veffels upon the faid River, fetting more than one Staunch of Water for the navigating one or more Gangs of Barges proceeding together, and keeping fuch Staunch fet for a longer Time than is neceffary to penn a fufficient Head of water for navigating fuch Boats, Barges, Keels, Lighters, or other Veffels on the faid River; for Remedy whereof, WE, the Commiffioners appointed, in and by virtue of *An Act of Parliament*, made and paffed in the 21ft Year of the Reign of his prefent Majefty, entitled " An Act for appointing new Commiffioners for continuing to carry into Execution the " Trufts and Powers of an Act paffed in the fourth and fifth Years of the Reign of her late " Majefty Queen Anne, entitled an Act for making the River Stour navigable from the " Town of Manningtree in the County of Effex, to the Town of Sudbury in the County " of Suffolk, in the room and place of thofe named in the faid Act, who are fince dead, and " for the explaining and amending the faid Act, and for other purpofes therein mentioned," DO in Purfuance of the faid *Act* and in exercife of the Powers and Authorities thereby vefted in us, ORDER AND DIRECT that in Cafe any Perfon or Perfons employed in the towing or haling of Boats, Barges, Keels, Lighters, or other Veffels upon the faid River, fhall at any Time hereafter fet more than one Staunch of Water for the navigating one or more Gangs of Barges proceeding together, up the faid River towards SUDBURY, or on navigating down the faid River towards MANNINGTREE, fhall fet more than two Staunches at the fame Time, in which Cafe the lower Staunch to be fet immediately preceding the drawing of the upper Staunch, fo that there be but One Staunch of Water penn'd at the fame Time, or fhall keep any fuch Staunch fet for a longer Time than is neceffary to penn a fufficient Head of Water for navigating fuch Boats, Barges, Keels, Lighters, or other Veffels on the faid River, every fuch Perfon or Perfons fo offending in either of the Cafes aforefaid, fhall for every fuch offence upon Conviction on the Oath of one or more Witnefs or Witneffes, or upon the Confeffion of the Offender or Offenders before any one or more Juftice or Juftices of the Peace for the County in which fuch Offence fhall be committed, pay to the Perfon or Perfons injured, THE DAMAGES; to be afcertained by fuch Juftice or Juftices, and fhall alfo forfeit and pay to the Informer the Sum of FIFTY SHILLINGS; which *Damages* and *Penalty* fhall be levied by Warrant under the Hand and Seal of fuch Juftice or Juftices upon the Goods and Chattles of the Offender or Offenders; And for want of fuch Diftrefs, the Perfon or Perfons fo offending fhall by Warrant under the Hand and Seal of fuch Juftice or Juftices be fent to the Houfe of Correction, to be there kept to hard Labour, for fuch Time as fuch Juftice or Juftices fhall order or direct, not exceeding Three Calendar Months.

Given under our Hands the Day and Year firft above mentioned.

JOHN FREEMAN, *Chairman.*

GOLDING CONSTABLE	JONATHAN STAMMERS
THOMAS SMITH	JOSEPH SADLER
JOHN LAY	WILLIAM GRIMWOOD.

SUDBURY: Printed by W. BRACKETT, Stationer, Engraver, &c.

An early printed version of a set of byelaws applicable to the navigation, dated 1790.

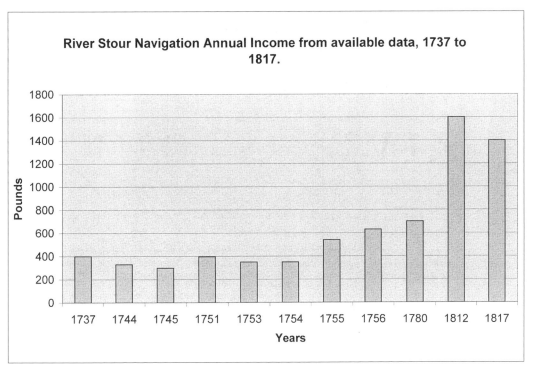

River Stour Navigation Annual Income from available data, 1737 to 1817.

Annual income statistics, 1737–1817.

trade coming and going from the ports at Manningtree, Harwich and Felixstowe was gradually becoming more reliable, these factors would clearly have ensured that the navigation was in a sound trading position. Geographically the situation was also advantageous: the agricultural economy around the weaving and market town of Sudbury creating a demand for raw materials and needing to export produce created a two-way trade along the Stour.

When in 1782 the new commissioners empowered by the 1780 Act appointed Golding Constable (father of the artist John and mill owner at Dedham) and William Strutt of their number to carry out a survey of the navigation, the result was that dredging works were carried out, more warehouses built and, despite the fact that the haling path problem remained unresolved, trade improved dramatically. A few available figures show annual receipts in 1782 of £700 rising to £1,600 in 1812 and £1,400 in 1817.[51] This clearly demonstrates several key factors: firstly, that a more consistent approach to the running of the navigation would have been beneficial to both trade and the relationship with riparian landowners and mill owners; secondly, that with the application of a certain amount of maintenance and development work, the trade on the river could have been optimised; a third factor must be that the navigation was indeed now demonstrably a well-founded and sound trade route; finally, that a period of growth could now have been realistically envisaged. The new commissioners would continue to deal with issues such as compensation of landowners for damage to riverbanks, and would report to the navigations proprietors or shareholders regarding maintenance issues. The increase in trade on the river that was apparent after the 1780 Act and subsequent survey works would have been encouraging to the proprietors and shareholders of the Navigation Co., and the building of the new warehouses is a testament to their increasing confidence. The period from the start of the nineteenth century towards 1836 can therefore be viewed as a period of growth and consolidation generally for the River Stour Navigation; the few figures that are available would seem to confirm this. By 1830 the navigation would have been in a continuous trading situation for a period of 125 years and the proprietors would have had the benefit of the knowledge and experience gained during this time. During the years up to 1836 the shareholders or proprietors had seen fit to lease the navigation wholly to a Mr William Jones to run on their behalf, but at the shareholders' meeting on the 14 January 1836, it was noted that the late Mr Jones had allowed the river to fall into a poorly maintained state, and that a committee of proprietors under a chairman and treasurer should now manage the affairs of the navigation. In September of that year Mr Edmund Stedman was elected chairman and treasurer by shareholders J. King, T. Jones, T. Musgrave and T. Hibble.[52]

Although the preceding years had been turbulent at times for Britain as a nation, the greatest period of social change was to come. At the end of the Napoleonic Wars in 1815, Britain was entering into what is now generally referred to as the Industrial Revolution, a period of considerable industrial development and social upheaval. At the start of this period the River Stour Navigation Co. found itself in a relatively healthy trading position, but about to face challenges that would have been inconceivable a few years earlier. By 1836 the Navigation Co. proprietors were undoubtedly aware of the industrial developments that were forging ahead in the country generally, in particular the development of the railways, as they sought advice as to the impact of possible competition from this new form of transport. As well as carrying

A gang of lighters on the Stour, laden with cargo and low in the water.

out a survey of the navigation in this year (see appendix 5), an engineer, Mr Joseph Cubitt, was charged with assessing the situation regarding the railways. In his report, Cubitt suggested that the Bill before Parliament concerning the Eastern Counties Railway would not be passed, and that the carriage of heavy goods by rail was not viable due to wear and tear on the infrastructure. Also noting a 25 per cent increase in the cost of iron, he concluded that the carriage of bulk goods would stay in the domain of the inland waterways. Unfortunately, Cubitt's conclusions would prove to be misleading, but having examined this report and the survey of the navigation, the company's proprietors would have been feeling more reassured as to the future. Further shares were issued to raise capital and most of the improvements that were recommended were undertaken, and this general optimistic and positive feeling would have been reinforced by a healthy financial position. It was at this time that Joseph Cubbit was also asked to examine the possibility of extending the navigation beyond Sudbury as far as Clare. A survey complete with costing was carried out and the final report was presented at a meeting of the proprietors on 7 October 1843. In the chair, Edmund Stedman read out the details of the scheme, which with all the proposed engineering works and land purchases was estimated to cost £30,005 11s. The scheme was destined not to be progressed any further; even in these buoyant times the cost was clearly prohibitive. However, by 1843 the value of £100 worth of shares in the Navigation Co. was £800, and in 1848, with the rail link between Colchester and London having been opened five years earlier, annual receipts for this period were now averaging £2,918 over an expenditure of £750.[53]

It can be seen quite clearly when one studies the only data available from the earlier years of the Navigation Co.'s trading (some of the earlier records are incomplete), the apparent considerable increase in income after the 1780 Act of Parliament.[54] During the period of growth and development that followed, the case for providing a continuous towpath must have been very clear, yet despite the fact that the navigation was by now well established and successful, this problem could still not be resolved. Resistance to change in this respect from the mill owners and riparian landowners was clearly still very strong, and failure to overcome this during these vital years, when the case for the towpath was at its strongest, i.e. that the navigation was a growing successful trade route of benefit to many and inconveniencing few, was to prove a big factor in the disastrous later years.

1849–1916

Whilst the proprietors of the Navigation Co. would have been well aware that the coming of the railway to the region was inevitable, the real wake-up call came with the opening of the Stour Valley line linking Sudbury to Marks Tey, and thereby to Colchester and London in 1849. As stated, it has been suggested that the Navigation Co. at this point offered to sell itself to the Eastern Counties Railway, and that the asking price was refused and a derisory counter offer made. The company's minute books give details of meetings with the proprietors of the new railway company, and at a meeting of the proprietors of the Stour Navigation on 27 October 1845 it was resolved that:

> The parties present, except Mr Jones and Mr Allen who dissented, and as far as the parties present can bind themselves, that the shares of the river be offered to The Colchester Stour Valley Sudbury and Halstead Railway Co. at the rate of one thousand pounds per share. Signed Capt. Francis de Visme, chairman.

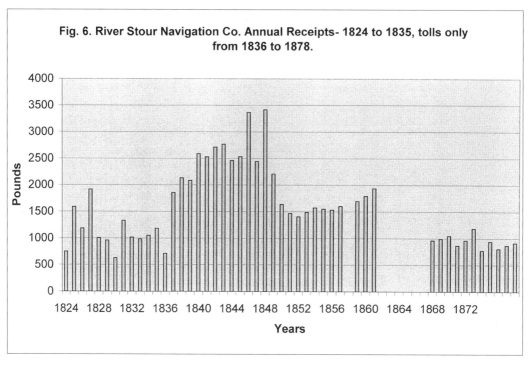

Fig. 6. River Stour Navigation Co. Annual Receipts- 1824 to 1835, tolls only from 1836 to 1878.

Annual income statistics, 1824–1878.

Present also at this meeting were Robert Frost Stedman, William King, Robert Alfred Allen, Charles Ray, Col. Addison, Thomas Jones and Edmund Stedman. When the proprietors met on 30 December 1846 the chairman, Edmund Stedman, reported:

> … that the Colchester Stour Valley Sudbury and Halsted Railway Co. having dissented from the provisions of the draft bill produced at the last meeting as not in conformity with their agreement, which was for the purchase of certain shares, the committee do not deem it necessary to make any order in the matter.[55]

This seemed to be the end of negotiations with the railway company regarding the sale of shares. Thus it is clear that the company did take the threat of competition for the transport of goods such as coal seriously, and at a meeting held on 22 June 1849, the chairman reported that if no agreement can be made with the Stour Valley Railway (regarding tolls, cargoes etc.) before they open their line to Sudbury for goods traffic, then the treasurer was to reduce the tolls charged for carriage of coals and slates on the river to 1s per ton. This was duly reported as carried out one month later. In this year the company also reduced their dividend to £15 per share per half year from the £20 paid the previous year.[56] The company was clearly bracing itself for its first serious competition since its inception in 1705. Physical improvements were now ordered to be carried out on the navigation itself at this time, including lock gate improvements and the removal of the older staunch locks, replacing them with six new pound locks.

Looking at the company's trading statistics in graphic form clearly shows the effect upon the Navigation Co.'s annual receipts of some of the key events discussed so far.[57] The period up to 1836 when the navigation was leased to Mr Jones, although more successful than earlier

This rare photograph shows a steam tug towing a lighter on the river. The Stour Navigation Co.'s steam vessel sadly only appeared briefly on the river.

years, appears erratic and unpredictable. From 1836 with the company now coming under direct control of a committee of shareholders who would have wanted a good return on their money, the highest receipts are recorded. From 1850, however, it seems that the advent of the railway meant that levels reached in 1848 were now out of reach. It is very interesting to note that the next eleven years, despite immediate competition from the Stour Valley Railway, is a period of *increasing* annual receipts for the Navigation Co., suggesting that the shareholders committee had actually managed to stabilise the fortunes of the business.

At a meeting of the proprietors in March 1862 the chairman, Edmund Stedman, perhaps anticipating the future, brought with him a model of a steam tug, but discussions of adopting steam power on the river were held over until the following month. These discussions were duly held and the estimated cost of £600 for putting such a vessel on the river was seen as a big drain on funds. Doubt was also expressed in the vessel's ability to accommodate all trades on the river, and further consideration was postponed until some more fitting opportunity. However, shareholder Col. Frances de Visme was charged with the task of examining such vessels used on the Grand Junction Canal. By August 1862, a Mr W. Jeffries was engaged to construct a steam-powered barge for £400 by the following Christmas. Two years later, after the death of Edmund Stedman, Robert Frost Stedman was elected chairman and treasurer of the company, and a further reduced dividend of now only £10 per share per half year was now being declared. A Mr Salter was to spend some considerable time altering and refitting the steamboat built by Jeffries, and trying to overcome the problem of finding suitable propellers that would work on shallow drafted flat-bottomed vessels without cavitating (drawing air around them from the surface, thereby impeding efficiency). He suggested a paddle steamer may be a better option, but this was deemed impracticable due to low bridges on the river. The project dragged on, test after test and trial after re-trial, until the idea was abandoned and the steam barge offered for sale in December 1867.[58]

By 1868 the company's annual receipts had fallen to levels not seen since 1833 and the steam-barge project, which if pursued more vigorously may have revitalised the company's fortunes, had been a costly white elephant. By now, any hope of making a convincing case for a continuous towpath was fading with the strength of the company being diminished, and tolls were now being regularly reduced in order to keep trade on the river. Until June 1869, there had been no toll on the river for general goods, i.e. non agricultural or 'heavy goods', and this loophole was now rectified. In 1870 Mr Salter was commissioned to survey the navigation, and on 14 August 1872, after the death of Robert Frost Stedman, Mr Elliston Allen was elected chairman and treasurer of the company, and immediately a schedule of the company's real estate together with a schedule of annual rents was drawn up.[59] The charts on the following pages show the respective volumes of the various cargoes carried on the Stour Navigation during the years 1851 to 1891 from available records.[60] Again it is very interesting to note the actual increase in traffic through the 1860s, particularly sacks of flour, quarters of wheat and bricks by the hundred. Although tolls had been lowered, examination of these statistics at the time must have given some encouragement to the proprietors of the company. Their difficulty was to find cargoes for both directions on the river, and coal taken upstream was the cargo that seemed to be in substantial decline primarily, as a result of competition from the railway.

In 1873 the company's growing problems were highlighted by the need to pass a ruling that no shares could be transferred without permission from the management committee. Falling receipts were also having an effect on the dividend paid per share, which had now fallen to £3 per half year. In 1881 the proprietors had installed a dredger that they had been considering to work on the navigation and the effect was encouraging. Whereas areas of the river would previously have had to remain closed for extended periods whilst laborious hand dredging took place, the new vessel allowed the navigation to remain open while it worked. This was a welcome improvement but the optimised efficiency that it created was not enough to have an overall affect on trade. The 1882 report by the Tolls Committee to the shareholders gives a good insight into the trading position of the company, showing trade centred in three localities: Sudbury to Mistley, Nayland or Wiston to Mistley, and Stratford or Dedham to Mistley. Goods carried from Sudbury to Mistley were bricks and malt, returning with coal, maize and barley. The coal trade was said to have dropped off due to a demand for low-priced coal from the Midlands, not procurable as an item of traffic on the River Stour. The trade in maize was seen as much improved. From Nayland or Wiston to Mistley the goods were flour for London, returning with coal and foreign wheat. From Stratford or Dedham the trade was the same. There was seen to be little intermediate trade except Sudbury to Nayland in wheat, and tolls generally were seen as too high. All heavy goods were now carried by the railway, but the report states that:

> … as there is a steamer running between Mistley and London, we consider it will be in the interest of barge owners to encourage a trade of this description which will give them back carriage from Mistley. We recommend all heavy goods (which we propose to call shop goods) should pay a uniform toll of one shilling per ton.

On 22 October 1886 chairman Elliston Allen reported that the trade in bricks was now severely affected by the development of rail routes into east and central London. The chart clearly shows the dramatic effect that this particular form of competition had on the Navigation Co.'s brick trade.

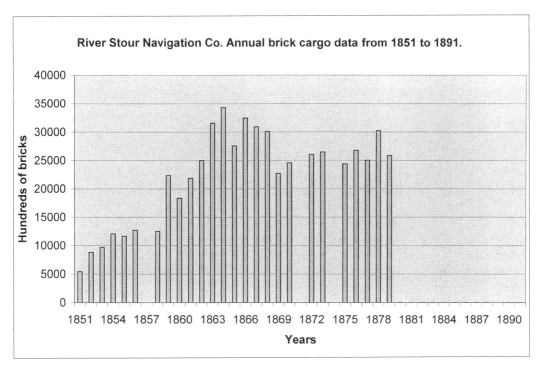

Brick cargo statistics.

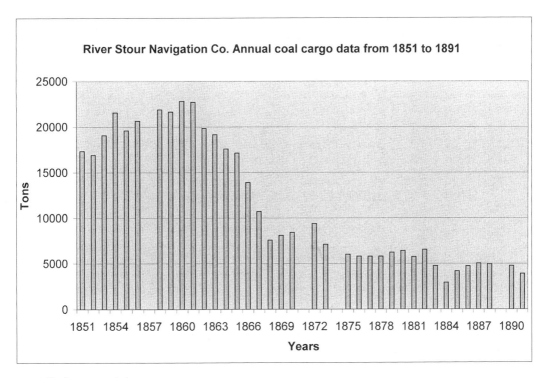

Coal cargo statistics.

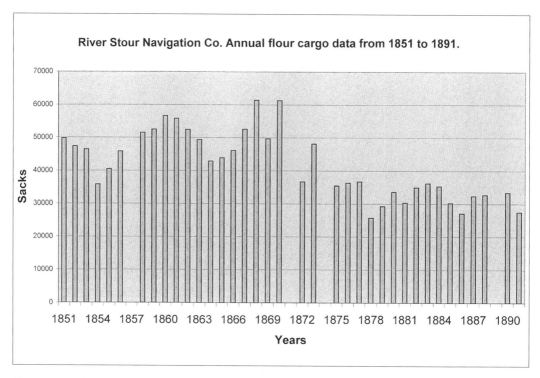

Flour cargo statistics.

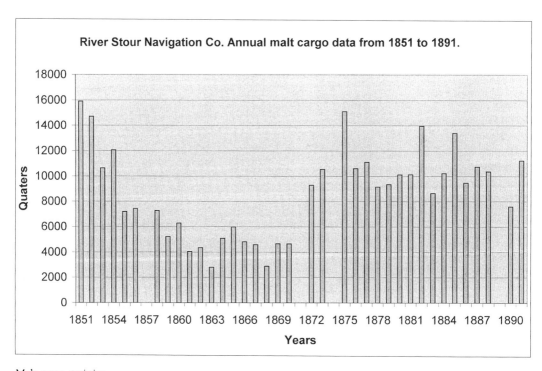

Malt cargo statistics.

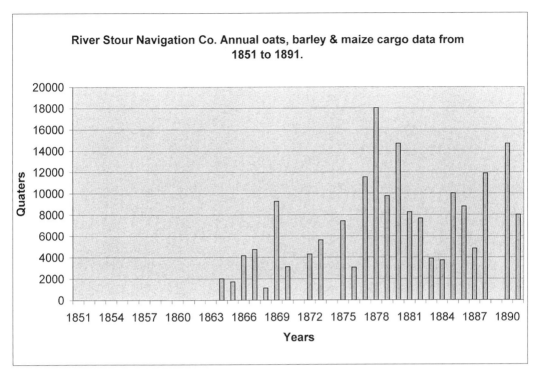

Oats cargo statistics.

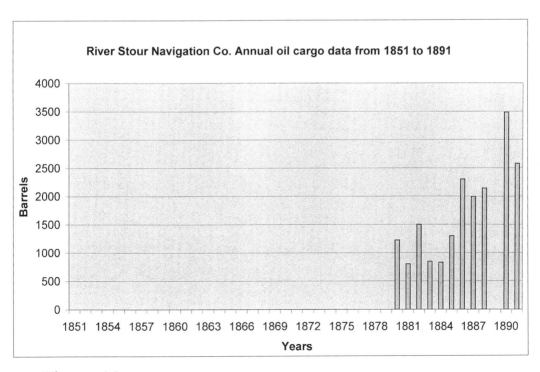

Oil cargo statistics.

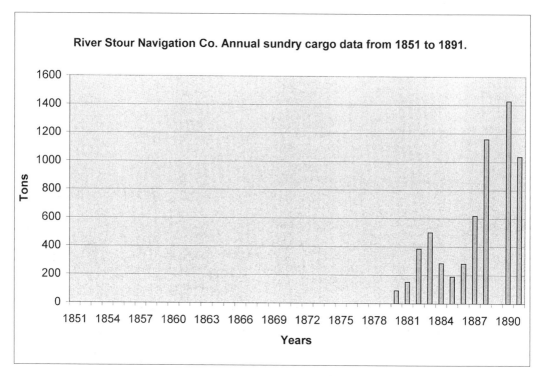

Sundry cargo statistics.

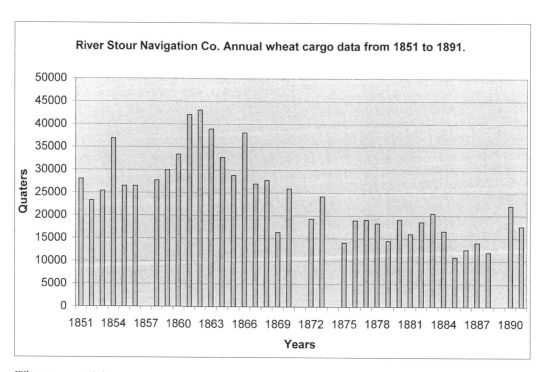

Wheat cargo statistics.

Lighters moving their cargo through Flatford at the turn of the century.

By 1888 the shareholders were clearly of the opinion that there was little hope in a revival of the company's trading fortunes and were actively looking to sell the entire enterprise. Negotiations with a possible purchaser came to nothing; however, hopes were temporarily raised with discussions of a scheme to link the Stour Navigation with the rivers Cam and Great Ouse but this did not come to fruition. The management committee were also now burdened with extra duties such as legal negotiations as to the liability for repairs to bridges and other property coupled with the new requirements of the Railway and Canal Traffic Act, 1888.

All of these factors began to weigh heavily and after seeking legal advice the Navigation Co., at a special meeting on the 15 November 1892, voted unanimously to incorporate under the Companies Act as a company limited by shares and to change the name to the River Stour Navigation Co. Ltd.[61] This action would relieve the problem of personal liability from the shareholders. It was this point, at the beginning of the last decade of the nineteenth century, when the proprietors of the River Stour Navigation Co., instead of enjoying reasonable returns, had to contend with increasing liabilities; that marks a defining point of no return for the navigation as a commercial operation. It may not have been obvious at the time, but with hindsight it was surely too late to put in place any changes that would have allowed the company to trade through the difficult times to follow.

The only lifeline was the company's property assets, and these were gradually liquidated to offset any liabilities. A severe drought in 1901 causing problems in the navigation and pushing more cargo towards the railways did nothing to help matters. At a meeting of the proprietors on 31 October 1907, Edward Oliver and Frederick Wheeler voted Percy E. Allen in as chairman and noted their regret at hearing that Elliston Allen was unwell. Finally at a meeting on 9 October 1913 with Percy Allen in the chair, attended by Edward Oliver, Frederick Wheeler,

"THE COMPANIES ACTS, 1908 to 1917."

COMPANY LIMITED BY SHARES.

(COPY)

Special Resolutions

(Pursuant to The Companies (Consolidation) Act, 1908, Section 69)

OF THE

RIVER STOUR NAVIGATION COMPANY, LIMITED.

Passed 16th May, 1918.   *Confirmed 6th June, 1918.*

At an Extraordinary General Meeting of the Members of the above-named Company, duly convened, and held at the Office of the Company, Great Eastern Road, Sudbury, in the County of Suffolk, on the 16th day of May, 1918, the following SPECIAL RESOLUTIONS were duly passed; and at a subsequent Extraordinary General Meeting of the Members of the said Company, also duly convened, and held at the same place on the 6th day of June, 1918, the following SPECIAL RESOLUTIONS were duly confirmed :—

1. " That the Name of the Company be altered so that in future it shall be known as the River Stour Navigation (Trust) Company, Limited."

2. " That the Articles of Association of the Company be altered—

   (*a*) By striking out Articles 9 to 12, both inclusive.

   (*b*) By cancelling the words ' In his own right ' in Article 74.

   (*c*) By cancelling Article 75, and by substituting therefor the following words: 'The Directors shall act without remuneration.' "

T. FRANK BOGGIS,

Secretary.

Dated the 17th day of June, 1918.

JORDAN & SONS, LIMITED,

COMPANY REGISTRATION AGENTS, PRINTERS, PUBLISHERS, AND STATIONERS,

116 AND 117 CHANCERY LANE, LONDON, W.C. 2, AND 13 BROAD STREET PLACE, E.C. 2—46911

Notice of the special resolutions passed on 6 June 1918, at the formation of the River Stour Navigation (Trust) Co.

Swimming at Pitmire Lock during the 1930s. By now the navigation was all but disused.

Reed cutters at work clearing chocked areas of the river during the 1930s.

River Stour Navigation (Trust) Co., Ltd.

37892

Great Eastern Road,
Sudbury, Suffolk.

Secretary:
T. FRANK BOGGIS.

11th June 1936

F.

The Registrar of Companies,
 Companies Registration Office
  Bush House,
   South West Wing,
    STRAND, W.C.2.

Dear Sir,   Your ref. No. 37892.

        In reply to your letter of the 10th
instant, I beg to inform you that the above
Company is not now carrying on business or in
operation.

        I am, Sir,

            Your obedient servant,

                T. Frank Boggis

10.6.36   Secretary.

12 JUN 1936

One of the last official documents from the River Stour Navigation (Trust) Co., bearing T. Frank Boggis's signature.

J. Frank Boggis and S.B. Barker, the Navigation Co. resolved to formally go into liquidation.[62] The liquidator, J. Frank Boggis of Sudbury, was appointed and in 1914 realisations were given as £124-10-10, disbursements as £113-19-10, and a balance of £10-11-00. Winding up was delayed however, the reason given being 'a public scheme is on foot for acquiring the undertaking as a whole.'[63] Interested parties were invited to a public meeting in Colchester to discuss a way forward, but this last effort to save the navigation was overtaken by international events as doubtless everyone's attention was now focussed toward the outbreak of the First World War.

From 1916 onward

Some time after the outbreak of the First World War, after it had become clear that the troops would not be home in time for Christmas, a decision was taken to scuttle the remaining barges that were laying idle on the River Stour, and to put down the tow horses. It has been claimed in some secondary sources that the decision to sink the barges was taken by the Admiralty as a precaution against them being used by enemy troops to access inland in the event of an invasion. In the absence of any evidence to the contrary, this can be the only reason for such drastic (albeit, as it turned out, completely unnecessary) action, as it is difficult to imagine any other motive for such a move. This action had little effect on the almost negligible amount of trade that continued on the river, but it did make the possible re-use of these vessels after the war even less likely. At the end of hostilities in 1918, the Navigation Co. did reform as The River Stour Navigation (Trust) Co. Ltd, with Frederick Wheeler as chairman, in the hope that the navigation could be maintained in some form. Limited use of the navigation continued and on 27 August Percy Clover was elected chairman of the trust company by those present, namely Edward Oliver, E. Green, Mr Lupton and A. Baker.[64] Nevertheless, the interwar years are characterised by a continued gradual decline in the navigation along with almost negligible trading figures and the last barge, belonging to Percy Clover, working as far as Dedham made its final journey in 1928. By now the demands for drainage and water extraction were putting pressure on the company, and a deal was made with the South Essex Waterworks Co. regarding their proposed Bill, in so much as the Waterworks Co. would rebuild four of the downstream locks and allow sufficient water for navigation.[65]

By 1935 the returns to the Board of Trade show the navigation as disused and derelict, and the River Stour Navigation Co. (Trust) Ltd met for the last time on Thursday 15 April 1937 at their registered office in Great Eastern Road, Sudbury. S.G. Wheeler and J. Frank Boggis attended along with chairman Percy Clover, with apologies for absence received from E. Oliver. The chairman read a letter informing them that, 'the company name would be removed from the register of joint stock companies at the expiration of three months from that date and therefore this company would cease to exist on that date.' The minutes of the meeting conclude with:

> … it is… resolved that the balance in hand, namely £18-3s-4d be paid as follows: - £6-6s-0d for legal charges to Messrs. Wells and Braithwaite, and £11-17s-4d (the balance) to the secretary in (lieu) of his salary and incidental expenses that may arise. It is further resolved that the books and papers of the company be retained by Mr T.F. Boggis, the late secretary, to be kept or disposed of by him as he thinks fit. Signed, J. Percy Clover, Chairman.[66]

Thus, the company was wound-up under Section 295(5) of the Companies Act 1929,[67] and over two centuries of commercial navigation on the River Stour came to an end.

eight

Management of the Stour Navigation

A general view

Since its beginnings, a good many individuals have been involved with the River Stour Navigation, from the numerous commissioners under the first Act, to those that had inherited or otherwise obtained shares in later times. This simple fact alone has to be seen as not always in the best interests of the navigation, as it almost certainly had a detrimental effect on the decision-making process and long-term view; put simply, it was a case of too many cooks spoiling the broth!

One characteristic that becomes apparent when studying the surviving minute books of the Navigation Co. for the critical years during the nineteenth century is the rather inconsistent attendance at meetings of the proprietors. In some cases the chairman and management committee may not have met in the same form more than once in several months, and important matters discussed in one month would be reinterpreted and re-discussed by a different line-up of proprietors a month or so later. For example, on 22 July 1865 the proprietors met to discuss, amongst other issues, the ongoing steam-barge trials. Colonel de Visme chaired the meeting, and was joined by E. Allen, R. Stannard, W. Stannard-Green, R.F. Stedman and W. King. The following meeting on the 24 August was adjourned, and the next scheduled meeting on 14 September was abandoned with no business transacted, as not enough were present to do so (only two attended). It was not until 13 October at the AGM that five of the six who had met during the previous July met together again.[68]

It also seems that the proprietors were from very diverse backgrounds. Col. de Visme, it would seem, had a military career and had inherited his shares from his father. Additionally, some mill owners and local traders are noted as shareholders as well as clerics, dignitaries and widows of former shareholders. This could have been a positive factor for the Navigation Co., with different individuals bringing their diverse experience to bear on the day-to-day problems and running of the navigation. Some moves to take this approach are evident after the Navigation

Co. came back under direct control of the shareholders, with the setting up and regular election of a management committee to run the day-to-day affairs. Other individuals were also retained for the practical tasks such as maintenance and collection of tolls.

Key personnel

William Jones is noted in 1836 as 'the late lessee of the navigation' and is described as not having kept up repairs, allowing a certain amount of deterioration to build up on the infrastructure of the navigation. Not much information is known about Mr Jones, although the annual receipts from his time in charge can be seen on pages 69 and 72, with some years showing a relatively healthy income.[69]

Frances de Visme first appears in the affairs of the Navigation Co. (then Captain de Visme) on 13 July 1824 as a proxy for his father James de Visme, at a meeting chaired by the then treasurer James Auriol Esq. He was appointed managing director and treasurer at a salary of £50 per annum in November of the same year, at the company's AGM held in Colchester by shareholders Thomas Gainsborough and John Thomson (solicitor holding proxies).

From this time up to 1836 when the findings of the Cubbitt report were made known, Captain de Visme presided over a period during which the Navigation Co. was bought back under the direct control of the shareholders via the setting up of the management committee and the required improvements to the infrastructure of the navigation were made. By making the comparison of these historical details with the annual receipts, it can be clearly shown that this episode was a particularly positive one for the company. In 1837 de Visme seems to have taken a lesser role with the election of Edmund Stedman as chairman and treasurer, but as a major shareholder he maintained an influence well into the 1860s (now as Colonel de Visme) and the ill-fated steam-barge trials.[70]

Edmund Stedman, elected chairman and treasurer of the company in 1837, oversaw the most successful period of trading in the navigation's history. This was a time when the company was at its strongest, but also a time when the first serious competition and challenges had to be faced. Stedman must be credited with introducing the steam-barge project in 1862, but the failure by his colleagues to see the scheme through to fruition would be ultimately disastrous. This local dignitary and philanthropist appears diligent in his duties to the Navigation Co. up to his death in 1864, but with the benefit of hindsight, he lacked the vision to make the crucial and hard decisions that were needed during this time.[71]

Robert Frost Stedman duly took over after the death of Edmund Stedman in 1864 for the next eight years, until his death in 1872. This period saw the steam-barge project getting nowhere, and a reduction in tolls, dividends and annual receipts.

Elliston Allen is shown as attending company meetings from 1864, just prior to the election of Robert Frost Stedman as chairman and treasurer. He takes an active role in the steam-barge project, and generally on the management committee until taking over as chairman and treasurer on 14 August 1872, following the death of Robert Frost Stedman. Allen's business interests lay primarily with the large family brick-making firm of Allen's of Ballingdon. Allen's owned their own lighters, which operated from their factory via Ballingdon cut along the navigation to Mistley. Elliston Allen took over the chair of the company at a time when a serious decline in the company's fortunes was imminent and as a precursor to this he seemed to look to the company's real estate as a lifeline, drawing up a schedule detailing all the assets of the company. Loans secured on property would help in the short term, but with the collapse in the brick cargo trade in 1886 due to the development of the London rail network, the situation would have seemed bleak. Allen remained at the head of the company through into the early twentieth century, and throughout this period the minute books show that the problems and responsibilities that arose were dutifully and diligently dealt with, despite the uncertain future.[72]

Percy. E. Allen was elected to the chair of the company on 31 October 1913 by Edward Oliver and Fredrick Wheeler, after Elliston Allen was reported as too unwell to continue in the post. A month earlier they had appointed T. Frank Boggis to the task of winding up the company.

Percy Clover was elected to the chair of the trust company on 27 August 1925, by E. Oliver, E. Green, A. Baker and Mr Lupton. He was the last barge owner to use the navigation, and the last chairman of the River Stour Navigation (Trust) Co. Ltd.

T. Frank Boggis of King Street, Sudbury, was the appointed liquidator of the Navigation Co. in 1914. The Boggis family were much involved with the Allen family and brick-making in the Sudbury area, and a company by the name of Allen & Boggis, lime and chalk merchants, had premises in Sudbury during the early part of the twentieth century. A letter to the Registrar of Companies in 1936 informing them that the company was no longer carrying on any business was signed by the secretary of the River Stour Navigation (Trust) Co. Ltd, T. Frank Boggis. He was the last official to represent the company before it was finally wound up.[73]

Decisions and decision-making

Many of the surviving records from the early and mid-nineteenth century concerning the Navigation Co. allow an analysis of the company's decision-making process to be made. It is important to note that the commissioners who were empowered under the original Act still maintained their authority as overseers of the navigation, but the shareholders were the proprietors of the Navigation Co., and as such were in control.[74] During the time that the whole enterprise was on lease to Mr Jones, we must assume that decisions were taken on a fairly unilateral basis. In 1824, with Captain de Visme appointed as managing director, it seems that the shareholders, dissatisfied with the current situation, wanted to regain control. This was achieved within twelve years, and the system of the management committee was instituted. Each year the shareholders selected from their number a chairman and treasurer who presided over a management committee, also elected from the shareholders. The management committee comprised some eight or so individuals, and was responsible for setting the rates of dividends and salaries, tolls on the navigation, overseeing maintenance and repairs to the company's property, purchases, appointment of retained staff such as the collector of tolls and river man, and approval of the annual accounts. The management committee seemed to meet on a fairly irregular basis, sometimes monthly; sometimes three, four or more months would pass before they met. Decisions on finance or policy were generally made by discussion within these meetings, but other decisions would often be made by taking advice from third parties such as engineers, surveyors or solicitors. An AGM was held, where the positions of chairman, treasurer and members of the management committee were subject to election by the shareholders present, or their proxy. During the crucial period of trading in the mid-nineteenth century through to the company's incorporation in 1893 and up to its final demise, this system of management remained, with members of the committee coming and going under the various chairmen, and with the appointment of Elliston Allen as managing director, after incorporation.[75]

How effective the company's system of decision-making was can be gauged from some examples of the process selected from the minute books. The affairs of the day-to-day running of the navigation are generally dealt with effectively with a common-sense consensus being reached by the members present at the meetings. In July 1881, after the effects of previous heavy floods had caused damage to the navigation, the managers put a dredger into operation, which by October of the same year was reported as working well to alleviate the situation. The meetings of the following year detail the formation and subsequent report of a tolls committee, which gives a very comprehensive view of the state of trade on the navigation at the time. This rather diligent approach is a characteristic theme running through the recorded minutes of meetings from the early nineteenth century onward.[76] Their problem arose from an inability to be galvanized into more decisive actions, needing imaginative solutions. In short, the system of decision-making worked well for the normal problems associated with the running of the navigation, but if a more contentious issue had to be tackled, it did not cope. No better example of this can be cited than the handling of the steam-barge project. At its initial proposal in 1862, the idea of using steam power on the navigation could and should have been seen as an opportunity to get onto a far more competitive footing. But the initial cost of the scheme, estimated at £600, was seen as dangerously expensive, and from then on prevarication and indecision on the matter seemed to hold sway. After much discussion, a less expensive scheme was sanctioned which attempted to convert an existing lighter to steam power, and this proved to be a waste of both time and money.

A more purposeful, well-informed and better-funded approach would have probably discounted the idea of converting a barge instantly and would have looked to designing a purpose-built prototype tug to work in the river. This initial reluctance to invest substantially in the new technology, combined with a lack of urgency about the issue, was to prove disastrous. The scheme was taken out of the hands of one engineer and put in the hands of another, with months and years passing with no conclusive results. It seems from the recorded minutes that no one was in any particular hurry with regard to this project, and clearly they lacked faith in it from the outset. Eventually, in April 1870, the resulting steam barge was redundant, and unable to be used or sold, was left to languish in the river.[77]

When making a critique of the Navigation Co.'s decision-making process at this time, it only really becomes valid if some credible alternative approaches are put forward. It has already been suggested that for the day-to-day running of the navigation, the management committee system worked well. Where it seems to have fallen down is when larger, more long-term and far reaching decisions were needed to respond to the challenges of increasing competition and a changing trading environment in the second half of the nineteenth century. The alternative could possibly have been to appoint a full-time professional general manager, to be in touch with the daily issues of the navigation and be able to constantly monitor the progress of work in hand. More importantly, as a general manager would be in a position to assess the needs of the business at first hand, the shareholders could then be advised of changes and improvements, and lobbied for the necessary funds to carry them out. Instead of outside contractors and engineers reporting back to a meeting of the shareholders on a monthly basis at best, a general manager would have overseen and monitored the work of these individuals or firms and made sure that they gave value for money on a daily basis. Had this system been in place when the issue of putting steam power on the navigation was first considered, the outcome may have been very different.

The minute books show that as well as employing a river man and collector of tolls, the Navigation Co. also paid a salary to the chairman/treasurer for his work and an additional yearly sum to him for his position as collector of tolls.[78] Perhaps some of this money could have gone toward funding a salary for a general manager.

Alternative strategies

Having examined alternatives to the decision-making process of the Navigation Co., some other commercial strategies are now suggested that could possibly have made a fundamental impact on the company's trading situation in the latter half of the nineteenth century.

Firstly, the issue of the haling path. As has been stated, this matter was never resolved during the company's lifetime. Neither the original Act of 1705 nor the 1780 Act managed to make provision for a continuous haling path and, consequently, the journey for a gang of cargo-laden barges was much slower and more expensive (not to mention arduous for crew and tow horse) than it could have been. The resistance to a continuous haling path from the riparian landowners was obviously strong, but it is reasonable to suggest that by the early nineteenth century a strong case could have been made to overcome this. The navigation was in a sound trading position, but was hampered by the numerous places (boating places) where the tow horse would have to be ferried across the river or be made to jump high boundary fences, as detailed in the Cubitt report (see appendix 5). The navigation could have been shown at this time to have been of great benefit to the local economy, and had the proprietors developed the case and lobbied strongly enough, a system whereby boundary fences could be maintained with self-closing gates or low jumps to allow a continuous haling path, could have possibly been accepted by the riparian landowners. Thus the journey for a gang of barges would have been made in far less time than before, putting the navigation on a far more competitive footing.

A second alternative strategy was the possible use of steam power. Along with the great artists already associated with the River Stour (Constable, with his depictions of daily life on the river and Gainsborough, whose family were involved with the Navigation Co.), one thinks of J.M.W. Turner's 'The Fighting Temeraire', painted in 1838, as being seen by many to epitomise the changes afoot during the Industrial Revolution. The grand old ship, the hero of bygone days, is being towed to the ship breakers by one of the modern steam tugs of the day, in front of a brilliant sunset. The proprietors of the Navigation Co. attempted to modernise and introduce steam power to the river, but failed. Had a different approach been taken, perhaps more money invested, and a prototype steam tug *designed* to work in the Stour been produced, this could have heralded a new era of more efficient and rapid cargo transport for the Navigation Co., allowing them to compete much more effectively with rail transport for bulk goods. Steam power is commonly associated with the development of the railways, but, in fact, coastal steamboats actually represent the first use of steam power in transport in the early nineteenth century.[79] Many steam tugs and boats were developed for use on inland waterways, and the failure of the Navigation Co. to establish steam power on the Stour must be seen as a missed opportunity of huge proportions.

Another strategy that could have been considered was the carriage of alternative cargoes. A key factor that proved to be part of the ultimate downfall of the Navigation Co. was the unhealthy dependence of the barge operators on certain cargoes. When these cargoes could no longer be carried competitively on the navigation, then in the absence of replacement loads, the barges could not operate. The cargoes chiefly responsible for this situation are coal and bricks. Another factor compounding the situation was that a barge needed to carry goods in both directions on the river to work at optimum efficiency, i.e. bricks to Mistley and coal back to Sudbury. When these cargoes were no longer viable, a good deal of trade collapsed. It was clearly not easy to identify other goods or products that may have been competitively carried on the river but sustained efforts to do so by the Navigation Co. may well have yielded positive results. With the industries of weaving and agriculture at Sudbury and the maltings and export facilities at Mistley, maybe more bulk agricultural products could have been carried downstream and raw materials, such as bulk fertiliser and cloth, back to Sudbury.

Company reform would have been another tactic that the Navigation Co. could have employed in the face of the changing trading environment during the mid- to late nineteenth century, by way of undergoing a fundamental reform in order to 'downsize' and become leaner and more competitive. Instead of a number of shareholders, all drawing dividends and some drawing salaries for running the company, one party who would then be the sole proprietor could have bought the shares. This individual proprietor drawing a single salary, and receiving no dividends on shares, would have been in a position to undertake any reform unilaterally. This reform, coupled with any of the other alternative commercial approaches already put forward, could possibly have carried the Navigation Co. through its difficult times. A sole proprietor may well have had the sort of radical ideas needed to tackle the problems, identifying new cargoes, using the company's real estate to generate new income, or even alternative uses for the navigation itself such as leisure boats taking paying passengers along the river through the delightful Stour Valley.

As detailed in the previous chapters, plans to extend the River Stour Navigation or even link it to other major waterways in the Eastern Counties have been proposed at various times. Generally these schemes have been beyond the reach of the proprietors, either through cost or simply because they did not have a powerful enough lobby with the authorities to push such schemes forward, particularly when the navigation's trade was in decline and when railways were seen more and more as the way forward for bulk goods transport. We cannot, therefore, view this as an alternative strategy that was readily available to the proprietors of the navigation, and as such it would be unfair to suggest that they should have progressed such schemes with more vigour. Clearly, they would have been more than happy to see the Stour Navigation extended or linked to other key waterways and would have welcomed the increase in trade that this would undoubtedly have created. Indeed, it is rumoured that when the Dutch engineers viewed the East Anglian rivers during the eighteenth century, they saw a system of natural waterways that provided the basis for an excellent inland navigation network if the rivers were developed and linked together. Furthermore, they could not understand why the British did not make more of this natural opportunity.

The River Stour after 1945

The years following the end of the Second World War were relatively quiet for the Stour, until 1953 saw the formation of the London & Home Counties branch of the Inland Waterways Association. With a mission to enhance and preserve navigable waterways, the association oversaw the setting up of local action committees centred on each waterway. The River Stour Action Committee began to research the history of the navigation and came to the conclusion that the Navigation Co. had unlawfully disappeared! Studying the original Acts of Parliament, they championed the cause of navigation along the river, and determined that this important piece of our industrial heritage should not be forgotten. They successfully took on angling groups and riparian landowners who did not wish to see boats on the river again, and in 1963 they recommended that the navigation be taken over by the National Trust. However, shortly afterwards the Inland Waterways Association set up the River Stour Trust Ltd as a registered charity to oversee the navigation. In a quite remarkable series of events, the Anglian Water Authority, at its formation, included in its preliminary Bill a clause that would allow them to extinguish *any* navigation rights as they saw fit. The implications of this were clearly

Cornard Lock lying derelict in 1956.

Brantham Lock, 1956.

Opposite above: Dedham Lock, 1960.

Opposite below: Flatford Lock, 1958.

Left: The hull of a River Stour lighter, prior to restoration.

Below: The floating Stour lighter, partly restored and tied up alongside the Granary at Sudbury.

Above: The restored Stour lighter at the Granary, Sudbury.

Left: The grand reopening of Flatford Lock by Lord Greenwood.

Opposite: The Trust's sign at Flatford Lock.

far-reaching and potentially catastrophic. When the Trust was made aware of this, they formulated a joint petition with the Inland Waterways Association to the House of Lords to have this clause removed. Francis Batten, on behalf of the River Stour Trust, stood in the House and when questioned as to who would have the power to remove this clause, he is said to have replied, 'you, my Lords'. This won the day, with the clause being removed by order. It would be easy to underestimate the consequences of this action, not just for the River Stour Navigation, but also for navigable waterways in general. To this day the Trust has brought about a considerable restoration of the navigation, and in the words of the late John Marriage:

> Since the Trust was formed, the local perception of conservation, industrial archaeology, water recreation and navigation has changed and now largely accords with that of the Trust. Whilst there is still some last-ditch opposition to its views, much of this sea change is due to continuous efforts by the Trust and the enthusiasm of its members. A feasibility study recently commissioned by the Trust and the Environment Agency indicates that there is no technical reason why full navigation should not be restored along the entire river from Sudbury to the sea…[80]

In 1977 the Trust began work on the restoration of a Stour lighter, and they have been responsible for the restoration of locks at Flatford and Dedham. With the help of the United States Air Force, the river at the head of the navigation by the Old Quay Basin and Granary, Sudbury, has been

Above: The restored Granary Cut.

Right: The restored and dredged cut by the former warehouse, now the Quay Theatre.

Opposite above: The new lock at Great Cornard.

Opposite below: The Granary, now headquarters of the River Stour Trust.

Above: View from the opposite bank of the Quay Theatre.

Left: The waterfront side of the Quay Theatre.

Above: Sudbury Basin, head of the navigation.

Below: The landward side of the Quay Theatre.

extensively dredged and restored. In 1997, with the help of funding from the private sector and National Lottery via the Millenium Commission, a new lock system was opened at Great Cornard, complementing the large stretches of the river that are now restored to navigation. Today the River Stour Trust is continuing to bring the story of the River Stour Navigation to visitors, schools and anyone with an interest in our industrial heritage. The development of the visitor centre at Sudbury and the formation of an archive there, as a repository for the Trust's records and artefacts, are exciting projects that are well underway at the time of writing. Guided trips along the river are available during the summer from various points, enabling members of the public to enjoy one of the most interesting, beautiful and tranquil waterways in Britain.

nine

Conclusions

The events leading up to and on from the 1705 Act of Parliament to make the River Stour navigable I believe indelibly shaped the future character and unique nature of the working river. The primary catalyst in this was the lack of provision for a proper towpath. This single important point which was unable to be dealt with effectively in the 1705 Act, surely created the most unique and idiosyncratic river navigation in the country – with almost daily occurrences of 'leaping horses' and lightermen 'poling' their vessels across the river with their horses aboard, captured in such a complete way by John Constable. In failing to deal with the towpath issue, the later 1781 Act did little to change this state of affairs.

Other Acts of Parliament empowering navigation works on rivers around this time managed to include good provision for towpaths. For example, the Chelmer & Blackwater Act of 1793 made good provision for a towpath on the new Essex River Navigation. Bridges enabled safe crossing of the navigation and tow horses were not required to leap over boundary fences.[81] It may well be possible to speculate that these provisions were included in the Act in light of experiences on the River Stour further to the north. Canal construction works elsewhere in the country were, by their very nature, able to include provision for towpaths as they were mostly 'newly cut' works, often including many innovative engineering features of their own.

As for lock-gate construction, whilst it has been possible to detail those that arranged, oversaw and generally bought about the works, the actual builders themselves appear to remain undocumented during the early days of the navigation. Later, during the nineteenth century, contractors such as Messrs Blunden and Mills are recorded as having worked on improvements to the navigation but there is no evidence to show that any predecessors of these later contractors took part in the original works. I think it is reasonable to conclude that these builders were local artisans working close to the lock sites themselves. Staunches and flash locks were common to East Anglian rivers but the pound locks on the River Stour were unique at the time for their lintels spanning the two gateposts on either side of the water. This constructional detail did not result from any effect of the 1705 Act but purely as a unique and clever local method of solving an engineering problem. The image of the River Stour lock lintel is now the symbol of the River Stour Trust, and is featured on every copy of their journal, appropriately titled 'Lock Lintel'.

When did the decline start? In terms of trading statistics the actual decline in the company's fortunes appears to have started around 1850, recovering gradually until the mid-1860s before starting a terminal trading decline from then onward. From a management point of view, whilst a successful system came into force during the 1830s with the introduction of the management committee, it seems that decline started in this sense with the proprietors and management committee's inability to act decisively with vision and commitment in the face of increasing competition during the 1860s. This decline was neither dramatic and sudden, nor an inevitable situation, but rather slow and probably almost unperceivable at first, with, as this research has suggested, opportunities along the way to halt or even reverse the decline.

Although the opening of the rail link to Sudbury in 1849 was certainly a wake-up call for the Navigation Co., it could hardly have taken them by surprise, as the development of the railways in Britain at that time had been an ongoing process for some years, hence the Cubbitt report (as discussed in chapter 7) instigated by the Navigation Co. in 1836. The coming of the railways was also the only recorded local development at the time to have an affect on the Stour Navigation.

The symptoms of the decline, as shown from the data examined, were primarily gradual falls in annual receipts, as a result of the lowering of toll charges, resulting in a reduction in dividends and of the share value. Ultimately, a falling of demand for carriage of cargoes generally and in particular coal and bricks is apparent from data shown in the charts. These symptoms are most apparent during the latter part of the nineteenth century.

The arrival of the rail link to Sudbury in 1849 was, in effect, a more or less direct challenge to the Stour Navigation, and the first of its kind in the company's history. The negotiations between the River Stour Navigation Co. and the Eastern Counties Railway (see chapter 4) clearly show that the railway company intended, in addition to providing a passenger service, to also carry a general range of goods, including coal, to and from Sudbury at the head of the navigation, which had previously been carried in bulk on the river. This form of competition was here to stay as far as the Navigation Co. was concerned, and was certainly responsible for taking cargoes from the lighters on the river as a result of lower carriage costs. It would take time for merchants to realise the benefits of changing to the rail system, but change was inevitable. When the rail network developed further into east and central London in the 1880s, the effect on the brick trade was dramatic. With the absorption of the Stour Valley line by the Great Eastern Railway Co. in 1898, the railway was now a major force in goods transports both locally and nationally, creating by then an enormous challenge for the River Stour Navigation Co.

In order to rise to this challenge and effectively counter the threat of competition, the Navigation Co. would have had to seriously examine the nature of this new competition and evaluate what steps they could take to regain an advantage. The navigation did, however, have a number of potential advantages over the railway, namely: a direct route to the sea via Mistley quay; the ability to carry bulk loose cargoes such as coal, grain or bricks in just one loading operation (even up to 50 tons per lighter); a greater overall tonnage capacity, as the number of barges that could move between one end of the navigation and the other could 'out-carry' a single goods train.

The problem was the time taken for a gang of lighters to make the journey, and therefore the carriage costs to the merchants involved. Had the Navigation Co. tackled this issue head-on, they would have been in a much better position to offer a viable alternative to the railway. Quite simply, they had to make the operation of the navigation more efficient. Given its existing advantages, if the navigation had implemented changes in its working practice and the journey time between Sudbury and Mistley had been significantly reduced, then it is reasonable to suggest that the River Stour Navigation *could* have offered an economically viable alternative to rail transport. This could have been achieved in two ways.

A modern lock on the Stour, showing the classic Stour lock lintel.

Firstly, had the Navigation Co. tackled the haling-path issue at the optimum time during the early nineteenth century when it was in a strong trading position and therefore when a convincing case could have been made to impose a continuous towpath on the riparian landowners, then by the time competition arrived from the railway, travelling times for the barges on the river would have been already reduced, putting the company in a much stronger trading position.

Secondly, by seriously considering the introduction of steam power onto the navigation. This is clearly the key factor that could have could have made the continued transport of bulk goods viable on the River Stour in the face of competition from the railway. The development of dedicated steam tugs pulling gangs of lighters along the river would have created a situation whereby large amounts of bulk cargo could have continued to be moved at a competitive rate and ensured the survival of the navigation.

The other changes discussed in this book such as alternative cargoes and company reform may well have made a difference, but not without the resolution of the key issue of journey time on the river. By the end of the nineteenth century, with none of these changes or reforms in place, and a well-established local rail network, the navigation as a commercial enterprise was beyond the point of no return for the foreseeable future, and trade after this time was negligible. Many other inland river navigations in Britain were to suffer a similar fate, but drawing comparisons here can be misleading, as the individual geographical locations and trading environments of each navigation seems to be dissimilar. Although commercial trade finished on the Stour with

By strange coincidence, some years ago I was involved with the examination of a nineteenth-century wooden sailing vessel wreck near the port of Brightlingsea, Essex. Amongst the dating artefacts that we lifted from the rotting timbers was a distinctively coloured brick. After cleaning, the words 'ALLEN' and 'BALLINGDON' became visible. The brick had come from Allen's Brickworks at Ballingdon, Sudbury, very probably via the River Stour Navigation, where it would have been transferred to the coastal vessel at Mistley.

the last barge unloading its cargo in 1928, navigation rights are maintained to the present day in the hands of the River Stour Trust Ltd.

Addressing the question of whether any blame for the Navigation Co.'s decline lay with the action or inaction of any individual involved, it seems clear from the evidence that it would be grossly unfair and unwarranted to lay this accusation on any individual person. The Navigation Co. had existed for a considerable time in the ideal situation of having virtually no competition, and had therefore more or less flourished during this time, despite the practical problems associated with the river. The company had continued into the period of competition in the hands of shareholders who had business or other interests outside the fortunes of the Stour Navigation, and although credible efforts were made to deal with competition, not enough could be done in time to make a difference. The day-to-day affairs and responsibilities were dealt with dutifully to the end, but the very nature and 'corporate identity' of the Navigation Co. was simply not capable of the sort of radical decision-making and harsh management that would have been required to bring about the necessary changes. Taking risks was not in the nature or interests of the shareholders at a time when financial risk-taking and industrial developments were going hand-in-hand throughout the country at large. As an example of how the shareholders outside interests would take priority, by the time Elliston Allen had taken over as chairman and treasurer of the company, bricks were an important cargo on the river, after carriage of coal had suffered badly. Most of the brick cargoes originated at the Allen brickworks at Ballingdon, and were loaded directly into the brick company's lighters at a wharf at the brickworks. A gang of lighters would carry enough bricks to build a small house, and bricks from Ballingdon cut went to feed the urban building boom of the nineteenth century as well as projects such as the works at Dover Castle and the Royal Albert Hall. But when carriage of these bricks became more cost-effective by rail, despite Elliston Allens involvement with the Stour Navigation, the brick trade on the river dropped dramatically. The Allen Brick Co. quite naturally had to keep their own costs to a minimum in order to stay competitive.

To summarise these conclusions it seems reasonable to observe that whilst the coming of the railway to the region in 1849 brought with it a competition for goods carriage trade, which the River Stour Navigation Co. could not ultimately overcome or even match, the company's demise was not inevitable. Had the major changes discussed been brought about, then it is possible that goods trade may have survived on the river for much longer, and possibly well into the twentieth century.

As to the fate of the navigation itself, it is now clear that navigation rights on the Stour have remained consistently since 1705, despite nearly being lost at the hands of the Anglian Water Authority during the 1970s. The navigation is now in good hands, preserved and protected by the River Stour Trust, who are working towards their ultimate goal of restoring full navigation between Sudbury and the sea.

Appendix one

The River Stour Navigation Co.: Timescale of Key Events

1705–1780

1705	The first Act of Parliament is passed that results in the first work to make the Stour navigable from Sudbury to Mistley.
c.1715 onward	Stour lighters are seen on the navigation for the first time.
Up to 1780	Documentary evidence shows lack of maintenance and poor working practices on river.[82]

1780–1849

1780	Second Act of Parliament passed appointing new commissioners to navigation, but fails to deal effectively with towpath issue.[83]
1782	New commissioners conduct survey of navigation.
1791	Warehouse building commences at Sudbury.
1806	More wharf-building work at Sudbury.
1836	New proprietors of Navigation Co. installed, survey of navigation carried out and advice on rail competition sought.[84]
1843	Eastern Counties Railway links London to Colchester.

1849–1916

1849	Sudbury linked to Marks Tey and Colchester via Stour Valley Railway.
1862	Construction of steam-powered barge authorised, along with river improvements.[85]
1867	Steam-barge project abandoned.

1892–1893	Resolution passed confirming articles of association of the River Stour Navigation Co. Ltd.
1913	Company seeks voluntary liquidation.[86]
1916	Barges sunk at Sudbury.

1916 to 1937

1918	Resolution passed to change status of company to River Stour Navigation (Trust) Co. Ltd.
1920	South Essex Waterworks Bill proposes to extract water from Stour.
1927	Revised Bill for extraction served. [87]
1935	Company seeks removal of name from register of companies.
1936	Company declares it is no longer in operation.
1937	River Stour Navigation (Trust) Co. Ltd dissolved.[88]

1937 onward

1952	Catchment Board replaces Waterworks Co., to be replaced by Essex River Authority.
1968	River Stour Trust formed.
1974	Anglian Water Authority takes over from Essex River Authority. Navigation rights nearly lost, but successfully defended by River Stour Trust.
1977	Stour lighter restoration project commences.
1975	Flatford Lock reopened. Gas Works Cut, Sudbury – restoration by US Air Force begins as a training exercise for their 819th Civil Engineering Squadron.
1980	Quay basin restoration complete and opened.
1990	Dedham Lock, now restored, opened.
1997	New lock opened at Great Cornard.

Appendix two

Glossary

Barge
: A large vessel, with no internal means of propulsion, designed to carry bulk cargo on the water.

Bothy
: A bunkhouse for barge crews along the navigation.

Chaldron
: An old unit of weight measurement for coal.

Chunker
: A drainage tunnel, often lined with wood, running across the river and below the riverbed.

Draft
: The distance between the waterline and the lowest point on the keel of a vessel, i.e. the depth of water required for the vessel to float.

Flash lock
: An early type of lock in the river whereby boards placed across the river would be removed when sufficient head of water had built up behind them. The resulting 'flash' of water would carry vessels over the shallow areas downstream of the flash lock.

Gang
: A pair of barges or lighters chained stem to stern, towed by horses and steered by the rear barge.

Haling path
: The towpath, or path along which the tow horse would walk towing the gang of lighters.

Keel
: The beam running along the centre of a vessel at the lowest point in the water.

Lighter	Another term for a barge, commonly used on the Stour Navigation.
Lock	A construction in the river for impeding the flow of water and giving increased depth, thereby allowing vessels to pass along.
Navigation	An inland waterway used by commercial boat traffic for trade, either artificially constructed, such as a canal, or a converted river.
Pound lock	A more modern form of lock featuring two sets of gates, a short distance apart in the river. Widely used on canals and inland waterways, particularly where steeper gradients are to be negotiated.
Riparian landowners	Individuals or groups owning land that includes the bank of the river.
Scantlings	Small beams, generally less than 5in sq.
Staunch	Similar to a flash lock, but a more sophisticated construction with a hinged gate or beam fitted to more permanent constructions on either side of the river.
Toll	The fee payable by the barge owner for transporting cargo along the navigation.

Appendix three

Table of Approximate Distances from the Head of the River Stour Navigation to the Tidal Estuary at Harwich

From Ballingdon Bridge, Sudbury to:

Cornard Sluice and the site of the lock	1 mile
Henny Weir and the site of the lock	2 miles
The site of Pitmire Lock	3.5 miles
Bures Bridge	6.5 miles
Bures Mill, Sluice, and site of lock	7 miles
The site of Wormingford Lock	9 miles
The site of Swan Lock	9.5 miles
Wissington Mill, Weir, and site of lock	11 miles
Nayland Weir and site of lock	12 miles
Nayland Bridge	12.5 miles
Site of Horkesley Lock	13 miles
Site of Boxted Lock and weir	16 miles
Site of Langham Weir and lock	17 miles
Langham Bridge	17.5 miles
Site of Stratford Lock	18.5 miles
Stratford St Mary Bridge	19 miles
Dedham Mill and lock	20 miles
Dedham Bridge	20.5 miles
Flatford Bridge	22 miles
Flatford Lock and Constable's Mill	22.5 miles
Site of Brantham Lock	23.5 miles
Cattawade Bridge and tidal sluices	24 miles
Manningtree Quay	25 miles
Mistley Quay	26 miles
Parkeston Quay	34 miles
Harwich Port	35 miles.

Appendix four

Schedule of the River Stour Navigation Co's Property, taken some time after 1866

(From EE 501/13/33)

Location	Description of Property	Tennant(s)	Annual Rent
Sudbury	Large Granary (part of)	J. Stannard	£12 – 0 – 0
Sudbury	Large Granary (part of)	R.& W. Stannard	£7 – 0 – 0
Sudbury	Cottage / Coal Yard / Granary (part of)	R. Barrel	£20 – 0 – 0
Sudbury	Counting House / Coal Yard / Sheds	Messrs Allen	£26 – 5 – 05s
Sudbury	Coal Shed	T. Ardley	£17 – 10 – 0
Sudbury	Coal Shed	Late T. Ardley	£17 – 10s- 0
Sudbury	Small Granary / Coal Yard / Sheds	Late R. Higgs	£17 – 10s – 0
Sudbury	Old Yard	Empty	(£17 – 10s – 0)
Sudbury	Cottages at Quay	Messrs Allen / ?	£10 – 0 – 0
Sudbury	Pasture Land	W. Berry	£15 – 0 – 0

Location	Description of Property	Tennant(s)	Annual Rent
Sudbury	Boat Shed	Nicholls	£10 – 0 – 0
Sudbury	Meadow	Friars Meadow	-------------
Lamarsh	House and Garden	E. Harris/River Man	No Rent
Lamarsh	Staunch Field	E. Harris/River Man	No Rent
Bures	Cottage / Country House	J. Dalton	No Rent
Bures	Granary and Coal Yard	J. Dalton	No Rent
Horkesley	Cottage	Swan/Ticket Man	No Rent
Horkesley	Stable (for use of barge horses)		No Rent
Brantham	Cottage / Stable / Coal Yard		
Brantham	And Lime Kiln	C. Tovell	£20 – 0 – 0

Appendix five

Transcription of an extract from Mr Cubbit's Report on the Navigation dated 22 June 1836

To Capt. De Visme and the proprietors of the Navigation.

London, 22 June 1836

Gentlemen!

Having during the last week in pursuance of instructions to that effect, taken a view of this navigation from Sudbury Quays to its termination at Manningtree, I now beg to transmit my report thereon.

The Navigation now being under different management to what it used to be at the times of my former visits, viz: in the hands of Proprietors whose interest it is to have the Navigation put upon the most improved plan of which it is capable and brought into and kept in the best possible state of repair, instead of being in the Hands of a Lessee whose interest it was probably to lay out as little money as possible provided the navigation could be kept open and left in a state that it <u>could</u> be worked at the expiration of a lease; I shall therefore proceed upon a somewhat different plan in drawing up my report, and instead of noticing every little defect or want of repair as they occurred step by step along the River proceed at once to the main features of the case, and state the general principles that in my judgement should be acted upon to improve the Navigation in the best manner and in the shortest time possible.

The greatest evil in this navigation is the uncertainty which obtains in the time necessary for a gang of barges to navigate it from end to end, which in some cases and with respect to some kinds of merchandize makes it more eligible for freighters to have recourse to Land Carriage than to employ the navigation; a circumstance which would not take place if the River were improved and put into such a state that a gang of barges could be sure of going at all times from Sudbury Quay to Catawade Bridge within 12 hours, and return the same distance in 14; a state of things which is easy of attainment with the advantage not only to the parties interested in the Navigation as Proprietors but also to the Land Owners along the River and to the mill property situated on its falls; all of whose Property must necessarily be improved by the best method of improving the Navigation.

This Navigation as originally constructed was effected by means of Locks and Staunches; Locks for the purpose of passing the Falls at the respective Mills and Staunches for the purpose of getting over Shoals between the Mills, or of surmounting the fall which might exist between the head of water of one and the tail of water of another.

Now the evil effects arising from these Staunches are too well known both to the Millers and to those who navigate the River to require any detailed description; backing up the tail water of the Mill above and letting down unequal heads and loss of water to the mill below, and other evils as regards the Millers, and loss of time and injury to property as regards the Boatmen and freighters and damage to the Locks arising from the same causes which augments the evil to all parties particularly the Millers.

Now to make the Navigation as perfect as the circumstances of a River Navigation will allow, all the Staunches should be done away entirely as has been frequently recommended in my former reports and on the following principle.

When one Staunch occurs between two mills it should be done away by making the Sills of the Lock above the Staunch to the depth of three feet below the dead level of the head of water of the mill below the Staunch and all the Shoals between the Mills be removed to a depth of 6 inches at least below the level of the fences or lower sills of the Lock above; the Staunch may then be taken quick away, and the good effect of the operation will be to the Navigation that Boats may at all times pass without let or hindrance; and to the Mills that they will have the uninterrupted flow of water in the River at all times and the benefit of all the fall taken up by the Staunches.

When two or more Staunches occur between two Mills the united falls of which are more than can be taken in by the above method, a new lock should be built at any convenient spot between the two mills, the lower sills of which should lie at least 3 feet below the level of the headwater of the Mill below, an overfall or Waste Weir should be put down at the Tail Water level of the Mill above, and a set of draw gates erected equal in capacity to the Staunch for taking off and regulating the water in flood times.

By adopting the above principle for doing away the Staunches removing all the Shoals and putting all the Locks in good repair the River would be Navigable at all times and even the shortest water times without the least let or hindrance: and the whole of this might be effected by the erection of three additional Locks, viz. One between Henny Mill and Bures Mill, near Pitmore Staunch which would do away that and new Staunch: another between Wormingford Mill and Whiston Mill at or near Fishpasture Staunch which would do away that and Widow Smiths Staunch; and a third between Nayland Mill and Boxted Mill at Palmers Staunch to do away that and Stour Meadow Staunch; two other staunches might also be done away by building instead of repairing two Locks viz: Potters Staunch by rebuilding Bures Lock; and new Staunch by rebuilding Dedham Lock: by which means all the Staunches would be done away.-

Another great object to be obtained in this Navigation next to doing away obstructions in the River is the improvement of the Towing Paths by obtaining grants for paths where from various causes none have ever existed, or having existed have for other causes been left to become obsolete by the lapse of time: it frequently occurs that the Horse has to be boated and the River crossed twice to avoid passing along a very short distance, for which if a right could be obtained a path might continue uninterrupted on one side for miles together and much trouble and delay saved in navigating the River, it would also add much facility to the navigation if a new towing path were made from Brantham Lock to Cattawade Bridges, the difficulty and delay attending the navigation at which part of the River at the time of neap tides and land floods is loudly complained of by the boatmen.

As regards the mode of carrying the works into effect I should recommend that the same <u>principles</u> <u>of construction be adhered</u> to as <u>formerly, but with better materials, scantlings and workmanship; for</u> <u>instance the Locks which form the most important part of the works, should be Timber Locks, but</u>

the Floors instead of being confined to just the space occupied by the Gateframes should extend quite through the Chamber of the Lock from end to end and the sides instead of terminating at about to thirds of the height of the Lock should be continued up to the full height of the Gates and finished with a Capsill, and wharfed up close the whole length on both sides of the Lock. The gates should also be of stouter scantling with more bars in them, and planked with sound Oak instead of Fir Timber; the paddles also should be made larger, and to fit better, and to draw with a proper windlass and chain in short with good materials and good workmanship the Locks with the above suggested improvements are the best suited to this kind of navigation.

Having thus pointed out the general mode of proceeding which should be adopted to bring this navigation into the most improved state of which it is capable at the least possible expence I shall conclude with a brief abstract of the notes made during my inspection, and which were to the following effect.

The report then goes on to detail Mr Cubitt's notes made at various sites along the navigation. (Taken from EE501/13/1, River Stour Navigation Co. Order Book)

Primary Sources

The National Archives, Kew, London:
BT31/37892, River Stour Act, 1705.
BT31/32579, indenture concerning finance of navigation, 1707.
BT/32580, Act of Parliament amending 1705 Act, 1780.
C103/12/3, report on conditions in Navigation, before 1780.
BT31/32583, list of members of Navigation Co., 1892.
BT31/37892/23, declaration of managers of the Navigation, 1902.
BT31/14429, Articles of Association of Navigation Co., 1893.
BT31/32577, application for certificate of incorporation, 1892.
BT31/37892/C, affidavit of liquidator's accounts, 1913.
BT/283/61, returns to Canals and Waterways board, 1889-1937.
BT31/37892/F-H, letters regarding winding up of Navigation Co., 1936–1937.
MAF/135/657, history of Navigation, unsigned, 1950?

The Essex Records Office, Chelmsford, Essex:
T/A 200/1(T/A 286), book of repairs on River Stour, 1759–1800.
T/A 200/2, Navigation Co. Account books, 1824-1836.
T/A 200/3, Navigation Co. Order books, 1824–1861.
T/A 200/4, Navigation Co. Account books, 1836–1868.
T/A 200/5, Navigation Co. Minute books, 1861–1892.

The Suffolk Records Office, Bury St Edmunds, Suffolk:
EE 501/13/1 to 7, Navigation Co. order and account books.
EE 501/13/10, Lease of Tolls.
EE 501/13/5 to 7, Navigation Co. account books.
EE 501/13/17b, Navigation byelaws, 1790.
EE 501/13/25, Navigation Co. Papers.
EE 501/13/28, Book of Repairs.
EE 501/13/33, Papers including Schedule of Property after 1866.

EE 501/13/36, Papers including Minutes of Commissioners meetings, c.1880.
EE 501/13/37, Papers from Stour Drainage Committee.

Additional primary sources

Selected papers, uncollated at the time of writing, from the River Stour Trust Archives.

Suggested Further Reading

Anon., *A brief history of the River Stour Navigation, 1705 to the present day* (River Stour Trust/National Rivers Authority – Anglian Region), 1992.

Anon., *The Essex & Suffolk River Stour: Sudbury to Cattawade Barrage* (Inland Waterways Association), 1974.

P. Bagwell & P. Lyth, *Transport in Britain – from canal lock to gridlock* (Hambledon & London), 2002.

M. Baldwin, & A. Burton, (eds), *Canals – A new look* (Phillimore), 1984.

J. Boyes, & R. Russell, *The Canals of Eastern England* (David & Charles), 1977.

V. Clark, *Stour from source to sea* (Colne Valley Print), 1979.

N. Cossons, *Industrial Archaeology* (David & Charles), 1978.

D. Defoe, *A tour thro' the whole island of Great Britain, 1724-26* (Frank Cass & Co. Ltd), 1968.

R. Edwards, *The River Stour: An East Anglian river and its people* (Terence Dalton Ltd), 1988.

D.I. Gordon, *A regional history of the railways of Great Britain: - Eastern Counties volume 5* (Atlantic Transport Publishers), 1990.

M. Lewis, *et al, Industrial Archaeology, Vol. 6, No. 3* (David & Charles), 1969.

J. Marriage, *The Essex & Suffolk River Stour Navigation* (Tempus Publishing), 2001.

H. McKnight, *The Shell Book of Inland Waterways* (David & Charles), 1975.

H. Moffat, *East Anglia's first railways* (Terence Dalton), 1987.

F. Rochefoucauld, (N. Scarfe, ed.), *A Frenchman's year in Suffolk* (Boydell Press/Suffolk Records Society), 1989.

F. Rochefoucauld, (N. Scarfe, ed.), *Innocent Espionage: The La Rochefoucauld Brothers tour of England in 1785* (The Boydell Press), 1995.

H. Rodolph de Salis, (ed.), *Bradshaws canals & navigable rivers of England & Wales, 1904* (David & Charles), 1969.

L.T.C. Rolt, *The inland waterways of England* (George Allen & Unwin Ltd), 1950.

L.T.C. Rolt, *Navigable Waterways* (Penguin), 1985.

R. Russel, *Lost Canals and Waterways of Britain* (David & Charles), 1982.

A.J.R. Waller, *The Suffolk Stour* (Norman Adlard & Co. Ltd), 1957.

T.S. Willan, *The English Coasting Trade, 1600–1750* (Manchester University Press), 1938.

I. Yearsley, *Dedham, Flatford & East Bergholt: A pictorial history* (Phillimore & Co. Ltd), 1996.

Suffolk County Archives, QS 912, transcript of talk given by H. Lott to Stour Valley Antiquarian Society, 1967.

Professor A.W. Skempton, *Transactions of the Newcomen Society*, Vol.29, 1953–54.

J.S. Hull, 'The River Stour Navigation Co.', Suffolk Archaeology 32 (Part 3), 1972.

Papers on steam barge and navigation by the late John Marriage, River Stour Trust Archives.

Endnotes

1 'River Stour Trust Archives', paper by John Marriage, June 1999.
2 Heights above sea level taken from V. Clark, *Stour from source to sea* (Colne Valley Print, 1979).
3 D. Defoe, *A tour thro' the whole island of Great Britain* (Frank Cass & Co), 1968, pp.521-533.
4 P.Bagwell, & P. Lyth, *Transport in Britain: from canal lock to gridlock* (Hambledon & London), 2002, p.1.
5 T.S. Willan, *River navigation in England, 1600-1750* (Oxford University Press, 1936), pp.25-26.
6 J. Boyes and R .Russell, *The Canals of Eastern England* (David & Charles, 1977), pp.78-79.
7 A.W. Skempton, 'The Engineers of the English River Navigations, 1620-1760', *Transactions of the Newcomen Society*, 29 (1953-1954).
8 Boyes and Russell, *Canals*, p.79.
9 The River Stour Trust Archives, River Stour Act (Copy of Act of Parliament, 1705).
10 Boyes and Russell, *Canals*, p.82.
11 T. Willan, *The English coasting trade, 160 –1750* (Manchester University Press), 1938, pp.24–27.
12 Ibid., p.25.
13 Ibid., pp.136–137.
14 F. Rochefoucauld, (ed. N. Scarfe,) *A Frenchman's year in Suffolk* (Boydell Press/Suffolk Records Society), 1989, pp.115–116.
15 Ibid., p.110.
16 F. Rochefoucauld, (ed. Scarfe, N.) *Innocent espionage. The La Rochefoucauld Brothers tour in England, 1785* (Boydell Press), 1995, p.29.
17 Ibid., pp.85–91.
18 L. Rolt, *Navigable waterways* (Penguin), 1985, pp.19-24.
19 J.S. Hull, *The River StourRiver Stour Navigation Co.*, Suffolk Archaeology, 32 (part 3), 1972, p.223.
20 RSTA, Act, 1705.
21 River Stour Trust Archives, disputes with riparian landowners are evident in the correspondence of the late John Marriage, founding member.
22 RSTA, Act, 1705.
23 Boyes & Russel, *Canals*, p.81.

24 M. Lewis, W. Slatcher, & P. Jarvis, *Flash locks on English Waterways, Industrial Archaeology, Vol.6, No.3,* (David & Charles), 1969.

25 H. McKnight, *The Shell Book of Inland Waterways* (David & Charles), 1975, p.34.

26 L.T.C. Rolt, *The Inland Waterways of England* (George Allen and Unwin Ltd, 1950), p.68.

27 Boyes and Russel, *Canals*, p.81.

28 Neil Cossons, *Industrial Archaeology* (David & Charles), 1978, p.343.

29 Anon., *The Essex & Suffolk Stour, Sudbury to Cattawade Barrage,* (Inland Waterways Assoc., London & S.E. Branch, 1974), p.4.

30 Boyes and Russel, *Canals*, pp.85, 86.

31 Ibid. p.86.

32 *Brief History of the River StourRiver Stour Navigation,* (Information unit, Anglian Water, Colchester Division).

33 Inland Waterways, *River Stour*, p.4.

34 D. Gordon, *A regional history of the railways of Great Britain, Vol.5 (David & Charles)*, 1990, pp.58–59.

35 Ibid., pp.159–161.

36 H. Moffat, *East Anglia's first railways* (Terence Dalton), 1987, pp.180–188.

37 Gordon, *History*, pp.160–161.

38 Inland Waterways, *River Stour*, p.27.

39 River Stour Trust Archives, quotations taken from picture card amongst assorted cards and images, gs/2854/ol, Royle Publishing Ltd.

40 London Canal Museum.

41 Boyes & Russel, *Canals*.

42 John Marriage, *River Stour Trust Archives*.

43 Boyes & Russel, *Canals*.

44 Boyes & Russel, *Canals*.

45 Boyes & Russel, *Canals*.

46 D. Summers, *The Great Ouse, The History of a River Navigation* David & Charles, Newton Abbot, 1973, p.158.

47 Bury Records Office, EE 501/13/10, Lease of Tolls.

48 National Archives, C103/12/3, Navigation Report, pre-1780.

49 National Archives, BT31/32580, Act of Parliament, 1780.

50 Bagwell & Lyth, *Transport in Britain*, p.1.

51 Boyes & Russell, *Canals*, p.83.

52 Essex Records Office, T/A 200/3, Navigation Co. Order books, 1824–1861.

53 Essex Records Office, T/A 286, Book of repairs, 1759–1800, Boyes & Russell, *Canals*, pp.83–84.

54 ERO, T/A286.

55 Bury Records Office, EE 501/13/1, Navigation Co. minute book.

56 ERO, T/A 200/3.

57 ERO, T/A 200/1-5.

58 ERO, T/A 200/5.

59 Ibid.

60 ERO, T/A 200/1-5.

61 ERO, T/A 200/5, National Archives, BT31/14429, Articles of Association, 1893.

62 BRO, EE 501/13/3.

63 National Archives, BT31/37892/C, Liquidators accounts, 1913.

64 BRO, EE 501/13/3.

65 Anon, *The Essex & Suffolk River Stour* (Inland Waterways Assoc.), 1974, pp.5–9.

66 BRO, EE 501/13/3.

67 National Archives, BT31/37892/F, winding up of Navigation Co., 1936-1937, BT/283/61, returns to Canals and Waterways Board, 1889-1937.

68 ERO, T/A 200/5.

69 ERO, T/A 200/3.

70 ERO, T/A 200/3-5.

71 Ibid.

72 ERO, T/A 200/5, Interview with Peter Minter of the Bulmer Brick and Tile Co.

73 National Archives, BT31/37892/C-F, Liquidators account and winding up of Navigation Co., and interview with Peter Minter of the Bulmer Brick and Tile Co.

74 A. Waller, *The Suffolk Stour* (Norman Adlard & Co. Ltd.), 1957, pp.12–13.

75 ERO, T/A 200 /3-5, National Archives, BT31/32583, Company members list, 1892, BT31/37892/23, Managers' declaration, 1902, BT31/14429, Articles of Association, 1893.

76 ERO, T/A 200/5.

77 ERO, T/A 200/5.

78 ERO, T/A 200/5.

79 Bagwell & Lyth, *Transport*, p.23.

80 John Marriage, *www.riverstourtrust.org.uk*, April 2005.

81 Dudley Courtman, *Report on Ted Pearsons talk to Chelmer Canal Trust*, April 2001, Chelmer Canal Trust Newsletter, Issue 17, pp.3,4,5.

82 National Archives, C/103/12/3, Navigation report, pre-1780.

83 National Archives, BT31/32580, Act of Parliament, 1780.

84 ERO, T/A 200/3. Anon. *The Essex and Suffolk Stour*, (Inland waterways Assoc.) 1974, pp.4-5.

85 ERO, TA/200/5.

86 National Archives, BT31/37892/C, Liquidators accounts, 1913.

87 Anon. *The Essex and Suffolk Stour*, (Inland Waterways Assoc.) 1974, pp.6-10.

88 NA, BT31/37892.

Index

If you are interested in purchasing other books published by Tempus,
or in case you have difficulty finding any Tempus books in your local bookshop,
you can also place orders directly through our website

www.tempus-publishing.com